Leadership as
LUNACY

Leadership as LUNACY

And Other Metaphors for Educational Leadership

JACKY LUMBY
FENWICK W. ENGLISH

CORWIN
A SAGE Company

For information:

Corwin
A SAGE Company
2455 Teller Road
Thousand Oaks, California 91320
(800) 233-9936
Fax: (800) 417-2466
www.corwin.com

SAGE Pvt. Ltd.
B 1/I 1 Mohan Cooperative
  Industrial Area
Mathura Road, New Delhi 110 044
India

SAGE Ltd.
1 Oliver's Yard
55 City Road
London EC1Y 1SP
United Kingdom

SAGE Asia-Pacific Pte. Ltd.
33 Pekin Street #02-01
Far East Square
Singapore 048763

Printed in the United States of America

Library of Congress Cataloging-in-Publication Data

Lumby, Jacky.
Leadership as lunacy : and other metaphors for educational leadership / Jacky Lumby and Fenwick W. English.
    p. cm.
Includes bibliographical references and index.
ISBN 978-1-4129-7427-1 (pbk.)
  1. Educational leadership. I. English, Fenwick W. II. Title.

LB2806.L84 2010
371.2—dc22   2010009972

This book is printed on acid-free paper.

10 11 12 13 14 10 9 8 7 6 5 4 3 2 1

Acquisitions Editor:	Hudson Perigo
Associate Editor:	Joanna Coelho
Editorial Assistant:	Allison Scott
Production Editor:	Veronica Stapleton
Copy Editor:	Nancy Conger
Typesetter:	C&M Digitals (P) Ltd.
Proofreader:	Dennis W. Webb
Cover Designer:	Scott Van Atta

Contents

Preface

Polonius: What do you read, my lord?
Hamlet: Words, words, words.

—Shakespeare (1623/1951, 2.2.191–192)

We began this book with a profound sense of malaise in our times. Somehow, something wasn't right. So many educational problems appear to be recurring, persistent, and intractable. In trying to discern why we were troubled we settled on the language used by educators, policy developers, politicians, critics, and parents in and about the schools in both of our countries—the US and the UK. We determined that at the root of the language used to describe the problems were some powerful images that were evocative and resonant. In short, we determined that the world of practice and action is anchored to a powerful world of symbols and sounds.

As we sifted through the phrases and linguistic patterns that ran through the rhetoric of both of our nations regarding education, we began to notice many similarities. We were especially provoked to think about the metaphors that are used to define education. Many imply partial solutions, or at least include images that contain solutions. We took note that when Yale economist John Geanakoplos began to develop a whole new way of looking at the financial markets and why they went bust, he was moved by a metaphor from Shakespeare's *Merchant of Venice*: Shylock demanding "a pound of flesh" (Whitehouse, 2009, p. A1). Geanakoplos thought that "a pound of flesh" was an image that underscored the importance of collateral in lending. When collateral was not adequate for inflated prices and lenders became uncertain, a round of selling commenced that began a downward spiral, where "falling prices and rising margins reinforce one another," that is, the "pound of flesh" (Whitehouse, 2009, p. A18). The use of this classical Shakespearean metaphor is credited with developing a new paradigm that explained the market forces few economists understood at the time.

We believe a similar tactic may be possible in education if we can understand how our use of symbols and language confines us to tired old analysis and worn-out solutions that we find replete in the laws and rhetoric of both nations, as they continue to struggle to improve the schooling of all children in their care. But first we had to deconstruct the most common metaphors embedded in education and why they were, at best, not adequate to the task and, at worst, toxic in their effect. This dismantling is the genesis of our book. We think it's unlike anything you may have read before.

The effort is anchored in a belief that education can enhance children's lives. That it does not appear to for many children is not the result of the conscious intention of policy makers or administrators. Rather, the pressures that shape and sometimes distort or impede children's progress are embedded in the foundations of human activity, in our social structures, and in our language. While politicians and school leaders devote much resource and attention to the daily practice of schools, language may infiltrate quite different attitudes and practices than those consciously intended. The mechanisms are not easily discernible. The language we use is like the air we breathe; we depend on it completely, but until it is cut off we are not aware of its importance. That it is important is a starting point of this book. Language does not just communicate our thoughts: it is thought. It shapes how we exist in the world, our morality, and our relationships. We use it constantly, creatively using metaphor to invite a kind of engagement. We create our world anew each time we compare one thing with another and invoke the tension of considering the similarity and dissimilarity between the two things compared. If we intend to disturb persisting patterns, it is through language that we must start. One of the greatest writers on the relationship between language, politics, and society, George Orwell, believed that changing language can change society. Going back even further in history, Plato (1973) depicted rhetoric, one form of which is the use of metaphors, as engaging not just the mind but also the soul. Our book focuses on language, and particularly on how metaphors are used in and about education and, more widely, what this can reveal not just about practice but about the soul, or the morality, of our education. It is intended to change thought as a precursor to changing much else. To improve our schools we must think about them differently. To do that we must describe them differently, and we must be acutely aware of how those descriptions lock us into predetermined solutions. Language is not neutral. It has a logic all its own, once it becomes text. We hope our readers will think more seriously about the words they use before they become text: in laws, rules, regulations, speeches, professional discourse, and editorial page soundings.

To achieve this very ambitious goal we draw upon writers from a range of disciplines and throughout history. We reflect a perspective from the US and the UK. We invoke images that may seem shocking, for example leaders as lunatics. We hope thereby to achieve to some degree a very difficult endeavor, and that is to influence people's thinking and not just their practice by hitting them in the heart as well as the mind. We leave it to the reader to determine if we are successful.

We gratefully acknowledge help along the way. Hudson Perigo at Corwin was consistently encouraging of a book that is somewhat "off piste." Alison Williamson cheerfully checked on references from the earliest literature onwards and prepared the manuscript. Working across the US and UK cultures of American and British co-authors has made each of us see things anew. There was more difference in how we think and how we use language ourselves than might have appeared at first. Working together has moved us both on. We hope that the book does the same for our readers on both sides of the pond.

About the Authors

Jacky Lumby (PhD, University of Leicester) is professor of education and Head of the School of Education at the University of Southampton, UK. She has taught and led in a range of educational settings, including secondary/high schools, community and further/technical education. She has also worked for a Training and Enterprise Council, with a regional responsibility for developing leaders across the public and private sectors. She has researched and published widely on educational policy, leadership, and management in schools and colleges in the UK and internationally. Her work on leadership encompasses a range of perspectives, including diversity issues, comparative and international perspectives, and leading upper secondary education. She coedited the *International Handbook on the Preparation and Development of School Leaders* (2008). Her most recent book, with Marianne Coleman, is *Leadership and Diversity: Challenging Theory and Practice in Education* (2007). She is coeditor of the journal *International Studies in Educational Administration* and is a member of the Council of the British Educational Leadership, Management, and Administration Society.

Fenwick W. English (PhD, Arizona State University) is the R. Wendell Eaves Distinguished Professor of Educational Leadership at the University of North Carolina at Chapel Hill. Formerly, he served as a program coordinator, department chair, dean, and vice chancellor of academic affairs at universities in Ohio and Indiana. As a K–12 practitioner, he has been a superintendent of schools in New York, an assistant superintendent of schools in Florida, and a middle school principal in California. He also had a stint as an associate executive director of the American Association of School Administrators and was a partner in Peat, Marwick, Main & Company (now KPMG Peat Marwick) where he was national practice director for elementary and secondary education in Washington, D.C. He recently served as editor of the SAGE *Handbook of Educational Leadership* (2005) and the general editor of the SAGE *Encyclopedia of Educational Leadership and Administration* (2006). His most recent books are *The Art of Educational Leadership* (2008), released by SAGE; *Anatomy of Professional Practice* (2008), released by Rowman & Littlefield; and *Restoring Human Agency to Educational Administration* (2010), released by Pro-Active Publications of Lancaster, Pennsylvania. He served as a member of the University Council of Educational Administration for seven years and as president in 2006 and 2007. Currently, he is a member of the National Council of Professors of Educational Administration Executive Board.

1

The Presence and Power of Metaphors

The metaphor is perhaps one of man's most fruitful potentialities. Its efficacy verges on magic.

—José Ortega y Gasset (1925, p. 35)

NOT JUST WORDS

Language and leadership are inseparable. Leaders traffic in language. It is language that defines problems and solutions. It is language that stirs the imagination, defines critical issues, creates collective consciousness in followers, and frames agendas for individual and collective action, whether proactive or reactive. Language is the ultimate form of the construction of symbolic power, the means to stir humanity to pursue conquest, manage change, right perceived wrongs, find compassion for the fallen, or confront impossible odds. And the essence of language for leaders is the use of metaphor.

Goethe once said, "All things are metaphors" (Campbell & Moyers, 1991, p. 286). How we think, how we make sense of the universe, is by means of metaphor (Beckett, 2003; Turbayne, 1962). Metaphors are not just a literary flourish used by those with a poetic turn of mind, but a fundamental tool that has been used by humans from the earliest times to shape

1

thought and action (Lakoff & Johnson, 2003). As Ortony (1975) says, "metaphors are necessary and not just nice" (p. 45). They are so pervasive and embedded in the way we think about things that we often don't even recognize when we have used them.

> Metaphor is an aspect of our lives so ordinary that we use it every day automatically and unconsciously and with so little effort that we rarely find occasion to remark upon it. Whatever our pedigree or education, our waking thoughts and probably our sleeping ones are shaped by metaphor . . . it is not—most decidedly not—merely a matter of words. (Mangham, 1996, p. 20)

FROM GILGAMESH TO OBAMA: METAPHORS COMMUNICATE AND CONNECT

From "I want to win that next battle—for justice and opportunity," used in the Obama presidential campaign, to the Sumerian epic of the warrior Gilgamesh, over two-and-a-half-thousand years before, ideas employed on leadership resonate through metaphor. In the epic, Gilgamesh is criticized for his love of war and for not acting as a "shepherd to his people" (Sandars, 1960, p. 60). Such images have been used as narratives and poetry "to transfer knowledge and elicit emotion" over the millennia (Goodwin, 1996, p. 487). The mixing of metaphor in speech and poetry is a potent mix of knowledge and emotion. Such an aim is even more critical in our own times for, as Booth (1979) observed,

> For the first time in history, a society finds itself offering immense rewards to a vast number of hired metaphorists, hired to make metaphors accomplish a predetermined end regardless of what they say about our character or do to it. (p. 66)

Bowdle (2005) has even suggested that television presenters use a metaphor in every 25 words of communication. Orwell (1961, pp. 353–367) has argued that the use of language both contributes to and reflects the state of politics. He uses the metaphor of a person who takes to drink because he feels a failure but then fails all the more, because of the drink. So policy makers and practitioners in education may use metaphors to conceal their failure to think and act effectively, but such language encourages a further decline in the clarity of analysis and action in response. For example, in describing Winston Churchill's leadership, Jenkins (2001) remarked, 'He thought rhetorically, and was constantly in danger of his policy being made by his phrases rather than vice versa" (p. 116).

Metaphors function positively and negatively. They have the power to help us create meaning and understanding and to improve how we lead.

They also have the power to manipulate, to shut down thinking, to deflect creativity, and to harm. Their very ubiquity, their indispensableness, lends metaphors great power.

This volume aims to make more apparent to all those with an interest in educational administration the positive, imaginative, and productive potential of metaphors and also their sometimes "hidden cargo of dubious implications" (Cornelissen, 2002, p. 267) and "insidious tendencies" (Van den Bulte, 1994, p. 419). The first aim of this book is to shine a light on the worldview of educational leadership created through the use of metaphor. A second aim is to explore possible new worldviews to be constructed through metaphor and to use metaphors to illustrate the leaders we need. We will argue that metaphors are not only about leadership; they embody the very act of leading. They are both subject and object simultaneously.

HOW METAPHORS WORK

To understand the power of metaphors we need to know how they work. The first phenomenon of metaphors is that they trigger an effect (Camp, 2005) by comparing two things that are both similar and dissimilar. The reader or listener is thrown into a state of momentary uncertainty, where the degree and significance of the similarity and dissimilarity must be considered. We are tilted off balance and find ourselves "exiles from the familiar" (Burns, 1972, p. 109). The term used to capture this mental state is "liminality," defined by Anderson (2005) as "the ambiguous condition of being between, at the limits of existing structures and where new structures are emerging . . . a transformative stage where a thing is in process of becoming something else" (pp. 590–591). A metaphor takes us into a state of liminality, where we work at creating sense: "It preempts our attention and propels us on a quest for the underlying truth. We are launched into a creative, inventive, pleasurable act" (Swanson, 1979, p. 162). The effect is greatest when the similarity is perceived to be not total but significant, so that meaning is created. For example, Barack Obama's generation is now described as "Generation Jones" instead of the "late baby boomers." Wells (2009) indicates that "Generation Jones" reflects the "yearning (or 'jonesing') of its members for the coolness of the 1960s and their parents' efforts to keep up with the Joneses" (p. 36).

The second aspect of the use of metaphor is that it constructs a relationship between the user and the receiver. Cohen (1979) believes that by using a metaphor the writer or speaker extends a kind of invitation. To respond, the reader or listener must actively engage and, by doing so, a degree of connection and, to Cohen, empathy and trust, is created. Such trust has the potential to be a positive or negative in creating acuity in the receiver. For example, Schapper's (2009) title, *Investing in a Girl's Education is Like Watering a Neighbor's Tree* invites the reader to consider in what ways watering the tree of a neighbor might be like the education of a girl, but not a boy. The reader has to create his or her own sense, imagining first what the attitude might be of someone watering a plant that belongs to another: generosity, foolishness, a community gesture toward the future? Then there is consideration of the tree belonging to someone. Does this mean that the girl belongs to someone in the way that a tree might? We have only touched the surface of the rich meanings, the sense making, the challenge to one's values created by this one image. The reader cannot receive it passively. He or she must actively draw on personal experience to make judgments in response and thereby be drawn into a relationship with the writer to learn more.

Engagement with metaphors has the potential to sharpen analytical acuity, to create new ideas, and to demand an active process of meaning making to understand what people do or how they relate to each other. However, metaphors do not always work in this way. Some metaphors have become so embedded in our language and thinking that they do not trigger the effect just described. Instead, they have become "dead" or "frozen" (Goodwin, 1996; Tsoukas, 1991). Cornelissen (2002) defines dead metaphors as

> those concepts which have become so familiar and so habitual in our theoretical vocabulary that not only have we ceased to be aware of their metaphorical precepts, but also have we stopped to ascribe such qualities, instead we take them as "literal terms." (p. 261)

When educators speak of "delivering" programs, or of "strategy," they are not generally aware that they are using metaphors. For example, in a speech by the former UK prime minister, Tony Blair (2005), outlining reforms that "will create and sustain irreversible change for the better in schools" he uses such metaphors as

> Over the last 50 years, state education has improved. And that improvement has *accelerated* in the last eight years.
>   But successive reforms since the war have not always *delivered* all that they aimed to *deliver.*
>   What is different this time is that we have learned what works. We have the experience of successful schools.
>   What we must see now is a system of independent state schools, underpinned by fair admissions and fair funding, where parents are equipped and enabled to *drive* improvement, *driven* by the aspirations of parents. (our italics)

The metaphors indicated here by italics are likely to be taken as literal by most; that is, listeners to the speech will not consciously engage with assessing the degree of similarity and dissimilarity and its significance. However, the message of central government and parents acting rather as machines, accelerating speed, delivering what is intended, driving, is evident once pointed out. It is schools and teachers who are to be driven and accelerated. The machine metaphor establishes education as a thing, not as people. While the metaphors may be dead in the sense of not registering as metaphors, they are very much alive in reflecting a worldview of education, a cultural and historical position. Dead metaphors have the capacity to shape thinking and values as much as those that are live. Such are Van den Bulte's (1994) "insidious tendencies" (p. 419).

WHY A BOOK ABOUT METAPHORS FOR EDUCATIONAL LEADERS?

Current educational leaders are beleaguered and overlooked; they do not have a voice in national policy debates and are very closely supervised as well. As a guide to leaders working in this context, the market offers many books with technicist and over-simplistic critiques and platitudes for improving education leadership. Such texts offer different frames for analysis, but on the human level may fail to inspire. The analyses and the implications for action that follow minimize the human variable. Rational dissection of leadership practice may fail to engage, reinvigorate, inform, or improve real practice. Leadership is about performance, and that is about inspiring and motivating people. That requirement contains more than working from checklists and management plans. It requires an interactive and dynamic presence, an ability to turn a key phrase in order to prod or inspire people to think beyond themselves.

We suggest that leaders can, by being more aware of the metaphors they and others use, add incisiveness to their capabilities and enhance their effectiveness. We note here that in the early career of the great French journalist Émile Zola, he made a deliberate choice of the bank of metaphors he would employ in his life. "I would bid farewell to the lovely lies of mythology; I would respectfully bury the last naiad and sylph; I would spurn myths and make truth my one-and-only" (Brown, 1995, p. 109), writes Zola. Instead, Zola turned to the sciences, and especially natural and medical sciences, for his metaphors.

Recent leadership theories, for example transactional leadership, distributed leadership, strategic leadership, and entrepreneurial leadership, do not tap into the long history of human engagement with leadership, which generally has been metaphorical rather than theoretical. For millennia, people have been profoundly interested in leadership, but the way they have tried to understand it is cognitively more sophisticated than through the right-brain-dominant, rational language modeling that has come to characterize our notions of leadership for, as Gandhi once observed, "if you want something really important to be done, you must not merely satisfy the reason, you must move the heart also" (Iyer, 1973, p. 287). This book sets out to provide stimuli in a standards-free zone and to encourage leaders to adopt a plurality of human responses, using both mind and heart in a comprehensive way. The book draws on a range of disciplines such as philosophy, anthropology, humanities, and literature to explore what metaphors related to leadership might mean.

We envisage a journey that draws the reader through historical and cognitive possibilities that are intended to inspire, resolve, confuse, and provoke reflection on leadership in education and what acting as a leader might entail. The volume will use metaphor as an heuristic, expanding on how the instability of metaphors found in policy documents, in literature, and in academic disciplines can be used as a tool for human development, locating leadership within a mythological universe, and not just a political and social one. We apply the framework of ideas specifically to leaders of schools, colleges, and universities, considering the relevance and utility of particular categories of metaphor to the purpose and practice of education leaders. The volume also dissects metaphors, both alive and dead, in the debate and discourse around education leadership in policy texts and current academic literature, proposing that while metaphors may have a positive purpose to stimulate reflection and inspire, they may also be used negatively to obscure, misdirect, and evade.

STRUCTURE

The book is structured into three sections. This introductory chapter establishes the rationale for the book and the framework for understanding what metaphors are, how they are used and their function in human thinking.

The second section of the book looks in more detail at how specific metaphors have been used and what they seem to be suggesting about how leadership works. Chapter 2 considers education leadership as a machine. The leader's role as inspector and quality controller is frequently described in mechanistic metaphors that stress adherence to procedures that are standardized and detached from human judgment. There is also a pedagogical machine, which supports not humanistic values and learning but instead the assessment of children's ability to perform as proscribed. This chapter considers why machines have become such a potent metaphor in relation to twenty-first-century leadership. Chapter 3 considers the role of leaders as accountants. The simple definition of giving an account does not begin to capture the baggage that has accumulated in our schools as a result of accountability measures. The chapter explores the reductive impact of a relentless pursuit of efficiency and waste alongside the compulsion to measure everything.

Chapter 4 examines the varied cultural understandings of the image of leader as warrior. Western concepts of warrior vary from Chaucerian rules of knighthood to twentieth-century codes of conduct or 'standards.' Late twentieth-century attitudes toward codes are reflected in education in the enshrinement of competitive behavior—a very different concept than some eastern understandings of warrior, such as the spirituality of the samurai. The influence on practice of war metaphors and the implications for how we consider the role of school leader are the substance of this chapter. Chapter 5 unravels the powerful influence of sports metaphors. While leadership in sports has much resonance with educational leadership, it also imports unrealistic notions of heroic leadership and a history of sexism. The chapter considers how far our policy and practice in education are driven by a kind of simplified and simplistic sports mentality which expects and extols the achievement of the sole leader or coach.

Chapter 6 considers education leadership as theater. Theater has long been a potent metaphor in relation to undertaking the role of leader, relating to varying audiences, and adopting or adapting a range of scripts. The chapter adopts two perspectives. First is the school as a stage, where there is an ever closer and more demanding audience influencing what can or cannot be enacted. Second is the school as staged, where administrators manipulate the actors, props, and scripts to ensure that the individual and corporate performance draws applause from a variety of audiences. Chapter 7 considers metaphors related to religion. The explicit moral, ethical, and spiritual role of leaders in education has been stressed for millennia. Many find in their faith inspiration and guidance that can be directly applied to practice in educational administration. However, the chapter also explores the prophetic nature of education standards and the priest-like use of ritual to embed ideas and actions that restrict rather than empower children. Quasi-religious rites are harnessed to shape leadership; for example, Calvinist notions of the chosen few and the wider Protestant notion that perfection is possible become expectations of educational leaders.

Finally, in this section, Chapter 8 considers the leader as lunatic. An exponential growth in bureaucracy has led to pathological behaviors evidenced in research throughout the world. The leader conceived as a lunatic obsessed with ordering, and with an obsessive–compulsive zest for perfection, may hide a lack of order and profound insecurity with burgeoning change. The chapter considers, among a range of disordered behaviors, sociopathic attitudes to faculty and to children, the fetishistic engagement with statistics, and other seemingly pathological behaviors. In the second section, each chapter ends with three subsections in which we consider what the metaphor that has just been explored tells us about the context, about leadership practice, and about leadership development needs, drawing out lessons for developing our leaders and schools.

The final section of the book looks at how metaphors and metaphorical thinking are embedded in recent policy and guidance documents in the US and the UK, and the implications for practice, for children, and for communities. The focus is on deconstructing manipulation and misdirection and exploring the range of devices by which people, leaders, and communities are persuaded consciously and unconsciously to pursue ends that may be contrary to their interests and values. The grand discourses in metaphors of leadership, those of perfection and equality, are exposed. The chapter considers how such metaphors may support aspiration and inspiration, but may also lead to a deluded belief in goals that are unattainable, thereby distracting from the reality of the current situation. They may be displacement activity, encouraging the appearance of striving for the positive when the action undertaken offers a means of hiding, and of maintaining, the status quo. Metaphors can act as a means to encourage articulation of goals and actions to achieve them, and as a means of supporting flight as people, organizations, and governments evade issues and difficulties. The chapter challenges the reader to imagine which metaphors might capture what we need in educational leaders for the twenty-first century, considering the criteria for the selection of metaphors with a full sense of human agency, rather than those which evade or function in a partially human way. The images of steward and of teacher are suggested as embodying care not only for the present, but for the future of all our children.

TOWARD A NEW KIND OF WISDOM

We have argued that the language of education is replete with metaphors (Marcellino, 2007) and that language both describes and creates reality (Giddens, 1976; Tsoukas, 1991). Our intention is to expose to leaders and to those who support them how "words beautifully woven may be a deceptive lure, a travesty of truth, an enticement to false judgment and immoral action" (Moss, 1993, p. 51). We also want to support them to see more clearly how metaphors have positively shaped and inspired policy and action and could further do so in the twenty-first century. Miller (2004) posits; "the dharma talks of the Zen masters' use of analogy or metaphor to clarify—little parables where every small object becomes a means to enlightenment . . . All these things become portals for a new kind of wisdom to arise." Our hope is that the exploration of this book offers a chance for a new kind of wisdom distinct from the standards-driven and seemingly rational discourses that currently fuel leaders' journeys.

In our preface, we explained that the starting point of the book was a deep sense of malaise and our belief that language is both a cause and an effect of our etiolating school systems in the US and the UK. Specifically, we think metaphors are at the heart of shaping our thinking and the actions that follow. We opened the book with a quotation from Hamlet where, in answer to Polonius' question asking what he is reading, Hamlet answers, "Words, words, words" (Shakespeare, 1951, 2.2.192). Polonius follows up with a query: "What is the matter?" meaning what is the substance (Shakespeare, 1951, 2.2.193). Hamlet imputes a second meaning: What is the trouble? This book is about the matter of education in both senses; we focus on its substance as refracted through language, and we explore the trouble it is in. We hope we have made a contribution to diagnosing not only the issues, but something of how we might begin to address them, rejecting superficial means such as a facile compliance with sets of standards. Rather, we suggest the more profound strategy of utilizing the intelligence and humanity of school leaders through reworking their language.

2

Leadership as Machine

Now, what I want is Facts.

—Dickens (1854/1990, p. 1)

RUNNING THE FACTORY

A widely known embodiment of the education leader as machine is Mr. Gradgrind in Dickens's 1854 novel *Hard Times.* Mr. Gradgrind urges his pupils to avoid all "fancies," such as emotion or imagination, and stick to learning useful facts that must be drilled into children in an unremitting stream of numbers and definitions. The Victorian values satirized by Dickens believe the school should be efficient, above all else, in preparing the young for a useful place in the economy and in society, and to avoid waste of time on cultivating useless qualities such as empathy or love of the beautiful.

The idea of the school as an efficient system that produces individuals fitted to a particular role is ancient. The *Agoge* education system of Sparta, which starved boys to fit them as warriors, was as much about channeling the young into their expected role by the most efficient means as were the Board schools in Victorian Britain, which gave children skills needed to become domestic servants and laborers. The twentieth century saw a new thrust for schools to become vehicles of the utilitarian, linking ideas of mechanized production to "scientific" approaches and efficiency to better equip children for their economic role. Beck and Murphy (1993) chart key metaphors reflecting how administration was viewed through several decades, from the 1920s, when they believe administrators were driven by the "principles of scientific management" (p. 14), to the 1930s, with its "conception of schooling as a business" (p. 23), and the 1960s, with a "technical and mechanistic" (p. 89) emphasis. Skinner, in 1958, writes of the development of education reflecting such a mechanistic approach. He is scornful of previous measures to enlarge education. By contrast, the time of mass production has arrived:

> There are more people in the world than ever before, and a far greater part of them want an education. The demand cannot be met simply by building more schools and training more teachers. Education must become more efficient. (p. 969)

Learning is described as a process of conditioning, rather like Pavlov's dogs, a matter of using the right training and triggers:

> The learning process is now much better understood. Much of what we know has come from studying the behaviour of *lower organisms,* but the results hold surprisingly well for human subjects. (p. 978, our emphasis)

The article suggests that efficiency can be achieved in schools by the use of computers and other mechanical teaching aids. Gradgrind would approve. The irony in Skinner's title, *Teaching Machines,* appears to escape him. The double meaning underpins our chapter as we consider the distinction made by Oberlechner and Mayer-Schoenberger (2002): "leaders as being—or running—machinery" (p. 11). The chapter reviews the nature of machines and compares schooling, as constituted in the twenty-first century, to machine-like qualities. It then considers how leaders themselves may not only run the school machine, but have themselves become like machines.

LEADERS RUNNING THE MACHINE

The machine metaphor is so ubiquitous in education that it often passes unnoticed. In the US, large city or county educational systems are organized in classic bureaucratic fashion modeled after machine notions, and educational leaders use time-honored and honed managerial practices based on ideas of efficiency possible only with machines. The idea of a human organization without conflict, because the presence of conflict is seen as a sign of a weak administration, is a classic example of the idea of efficiency embodied in a machine, which has come to dominate our norms regarding the "effectiveness" of leadership.

The *Concise Oxford Dictionary* (Fowler & Fowler, 1964) defines a machine as "an apparatus for applying mechanical power, having several parts each with a definite function" (p. 731). The features of an idealized machine are defined below:

- It is constructed so that each part performs a specific function.
- The apparatus can continue to function as long as fuel lasts, without any intelligence directing it.
- It will function with a consistently repeated action.
- It will produce identical outputs.
- It produces faster than can be achieved by human or animal means.

When these same principles are applied to bureaucratic structures, including school systems, the type of organization that emerges has clear patterns of authority, and that authority is centralized, with hierarchically arranged offices; a unity of command in which every person has a boss and only one boss, line officers to carry out orders, and staff officers to provide support to the line. The individual interests of persons in the structure become subordinate to the whole organization, and work specialization is encouraged in order to attain efficiency. This type of military structure was created by Frederick the Great in building his army into a formidable fighting machine (Morgan, 1986, p. 26).

The industrial revolution and its demands for planning to carry out the requirements for the production of standardized goods found Frederick the Great's military machine structure perfectly suited to the task. Standardized goods required strict obedience, no creativity, and uniformity prized above all else. Notes Morgan (1986):

> The motions of the organizational structure thus produced are made to operate as precisely as possible through patterns of authority, e.g., in terms of job responsibilities and the right to give orders and to exact obedience. (p. 27)

Henry Ford was the first to create the modern assembly line in America, but the monotony of work caused by mechanization resulted in a rise in employee turnover to 380% per year. He was only able to find stability when he decided to pay his workers five dollars a day, an incredibly high wage for the time. But Ford broached no questioning of his authority. Brehony and Deem (2005) characterize the Fordist mode:

> Fordist organizations were alleged to produce standardised goods by means of inflexible production processes under Taylorist scientific management, where each stage of the labour process was broken down into small pieces done by different workers, carefully regulated by time and management surveillance. (pp. 398–399)

Fordism, therefore, specifically links mechanical functions to management principles, through invoking Taylor, the early theorist on scientific management. It was Taylor who once scolded a worker in his plant by remarking, "You are not supposed to think. There are other people paid for thinking around here" (Morgan, 1986, p. 32). Taking each of the factors bulleted above, we explore the machine metaphor by proffering ideas on how the leadership of education can be seen as similar or dissimilar to a machine.

Assembling the Parts

There has been a considerable diversification in the people who are involved in the education endeavor. With the advent of the Children's Act (2004) in the UK, education has been enlarged to become the Children's Service in each district, which integrates a wider range of professionals. As a consequence, the school leader must work with social workers and health care specialists, among others, on the school site. The Act's intention was

> to encourage integrated planning, commissioning, and delivery of children's services as well as improve multidisciplinary working, remove duplication, increase accountability and improve the coordination of individual and joint inspections in local authorities. (Department for Children, Schools and Families, 2009a)

Those concerned with, for example, the mental or sexual health of young people or their safety provide specialist services as part of an overall team. Additionally, workforce remodeling in the UK has reshaped the role of staff engaged with instruction in the classroom. Brehony and Deem (2005) consider one outcome of the reform process, charting a 91% increase between 1996 and 2003 in the number of staff in England who support education but are not teachers, such as teaching assistants, youth workers, and technicians. The ever-growing number of such staff impacts practice, so that teachers and leaders spend an increasing amount of their time supervising the team rather than teaching. Levin (2002) explores similar changes in US community colleges, with a considerable increase in the use of part-time faculty and administrators to the extent that, in some colleges, faculty have become the minority within the workforce.

Education workers have become intricate parts assembled with other roles to function together, subject to regulation and surveillance. This has always been the case to some degree: Administrators lead teams. However, it is the substantial change in the proportion of different kinds of worker, and the greater range of training and qualifications within the school workforce, that has led to a significant modification. This is not to suggest that there are not the best intentions behind national policies, or that there are no outcomes that benefit children and teachers. However, the machine metaphor causes us to consider the values underpinning action and the implications for the system, longer term. The plethora of quasiprofessional and noneducation professionals directly involved in children's education has replaced a more traditional model where the principal leads a workforce that is made up primarily of qualified professional teachers. There are parallels with mechanized production processes, as Womack, Jones, and Roos (1990) describe in their consideration of changes in organizations:

> Mass-producers began to use narrowly skilled professionals to design products made by unskilled or semiskilled workers tending expensive, single-purpose machines. These churned out standardized products in very high volume. (p. 1)

Changes in the UK education workforce evidence a larger number and proportion of both the narrowly skilled (healthcare workers, youth workers) and the semiskilled (teaching assistants) as compared to the skills of teachers. The net result of a mass product workforce was that many employees found work boring. While not all who work in school feel this way, there is evidence of dissatisfaction or dismay at the de-professionalization of teaching and a fear that teachers are becoming technicians who administer defined instruction programs and tests, rather than functioning as creative professionals (Gunter & Butt, 2005; Whitty, 1994; Wilkinson, 2005; Yarker, 2005). There is also evidence that the changes outlined have considerable impact on the work of the principal (Gunter, 2004). For example, the traditional role of *primus inter pares,* first among equals, cannot hold if the workforce is not primarily faculty whose education, qualifications, and experience are equivalent.

A Directing Intelligence

The role of school leader is also metamorphosing, as more people contribute to the function. In the Netherlands there are "more schools" (p. 4) (Collins, Ireson, Stubbs, Nash, & Burnside, 2006), where one principal heads more than one school. Other models are also evident:

1. Federations of schools with one board and a superintendent.

2. Federations of schools with one board, no superintendent, and several principals or more school heads.

3. Federations of schools with one board, without being overseen by a superintendent or more school heads. (p. 4)

The machine-like manipulation of various parts allows different kinds of machine models where, in some cases, there is no principal or superintendent at all; the school machine runs with only a shared board.

In England and elsewhere, head teacher roles are being developed into shared headship or leaders of more than one school. Glatter and Harvey (2006) found three different variations:

- Executive heads, who have responsibility for more than one school.
- Federations, in which groups of schools agree formally to work together in part through structural changes.
- Coheadships, where two heads jobshare the leadership of the school, or dual headship, where two full-time heads lead the school. (pp. 3–4)

The primacy of the principal or head teacher whose role was to support education by establishing a vision and ethical/spiritual and instructional leadership is eroded. In some parts of the world, the role appears redundant and the principal is primarily an operational administrator. The machine, having been set in motion, can run without a principal's guiding intelligence. The absence of such a steer is predicated on an efficient school machine functioning by prescribed methods.

Functioning Consistently

The twentieth century saw a post-Second World War thrust to improve industrial production, through quality systems designed to boost volume, consistency, and fitness of outcomes. The increasing use of computers was a second strategy. Consistency of function, a key element of machines, is considered here, first by exploring the nature of quality systems in education, and second by the use of computers as a pedagogic tool.

Quality

The language of industrial quality systems resonates throughout the development of twentieth- and twenty-first-century education. Milliken and Colohan (2004) see "efficiency" as key in the 1980s, quality in the 1990s, and quality control linked to accountability "the management philosophy of the new millennium" (p. 381). Just what the concept of quality implies is highly contested, often reflecting a range of formulations by gurus rather than resulting from empirically based investigation. Deming (1982), Crosby (1984), and Ishikawa (1985) are some of the most widely cited and, despite differences between them, all reflect the desire to achieve machine-like attributes such as uniformity of output at lowered cost and meeting specified requirements.

The ideology of machine perfection has manifested itself in a variety of ways in educational development. First, there are process quality systems. These emphasize consistent procedures, rather than systems, which Sallis (1996) calls transformational, and which use human creativity as the basis of improvement. Second, there is school effectiveness research generating variously recommended factors that lead to improvement. Both have similar goals to those of quality systems in industry: harnessing machine-like qualities to achieve improved and consistent standards.

In the UK, the White Paper *Education and Training for the 21st Century* (Department for Education and Skills, 1991) recognized three levels of quality: quality control, examinations and validation, and external assessment. The influence on practice of the resulting policy has been profound; the curriculum and its outcomes are delineated in the National Curriculum. Teachers are required to provide detailed lesson plans; to monitor and record their interaction with students, the students' work, and achievements; and to self-evaluate relentlessly. The skills teachers and administrators must bring to bear are proscribed by national sets of competencies, and their leadership or instruction is assessed by performance management measures. Testing of students takes place at levels of frequency that have seriously alarmed some parents and academics (Barber, 1991; Broadfoot, 1991; Connor, 2003; Locker & Cropley, 2004). External inspections have been accepted as an inevitable facet of leading a school. Education is suffused with quality assurance—that is, "consistently meeting product specification or getting things right first time, every time"—and quality control—"the detection and the elimination of components or final products which are not up to standard" (Sallis, 1996, p. 19). The UK government points to a rise in examination results as the justification for the quasimechanization of education (Kelly, 2005). Others question the cost: the loss of control by administrators, the stress experienced by both faculty and students, and the dehumanizing of education (O'Connor, 2008). Considering schools as machines demands we evaluate not only the power and effectiveness of machines, but their literally inhuman disregard for any phenomenon or factor in the environment that might be relevant to their input or output. They just keep going, even when to do so destroys the materials used or what is in their path. The vital element of what Hawkridge (2003) terms the "human in the machine" (p. 15) may be lost. The ghost of Gradgrind is glimpsed in our classrooms both in the mechanization of processes and in the reductive aims of education.

Effectiveness Research

Many researchers of school effectiveness would hotly deny that their approach is reductionist or machine-like. However, their generally statistical search for the factors that lead to success, however defined, has a flavor of machine-like efficiency. Wrigley (2004) suggests that the resulting prescriptions are methodologically and contextually reductive due to ℯ a mechanistic causality, that is, a belief in one-to-one correspondences, and

ℯ a failure to examine environmental influences and effects when tracing causal relationships within a system. (p. 229)

Ever more sophisticated models are developed, with complex moderating and mediating variables (Leithwood & Jantzi, 2005b), in an attempt to define the leadership behaviors that will achieve the desired goal, usually an improvement in test results. Consider, for example, Sammons, Hillman, and Mortimore's (1995) wide-ranging review of the UK research, which arrived at a list of eleven factors for effective schools, the last of which was that the school must be a learning organization; or Mulford and Silins's (2003) use of data from two Australian states to identify four dimensions that together define organizational learning in high schools:

ℯ a trusting and collaborative climate,

ℯ a shared and monitored mission,

ℯ taking initiatives and risks, and

ℯ professional development. (adapted from Mulford & Silins, 2003, p. 178)

They conclude that leadership is critical to achieve these elements. The lists from both studies and from others (Leithwood, Day, Sammons, Harris, & Hopkins, 2006), while founded on rigorous research, nevertheless present factors that are not novel and are inexact in concept. For example, trust and collaboration are widely thought to be key characteristics of successful leadership, but what they are and how they can be achieved is no clearer for the terms being put in a list. Wrigley (2004) accuses effectiveness research of failing to engage with why ideas are popular in a particular era. The underlying motivation of effectiveness research appears to be very much in line with the thrust toward machine-like functioning, defining the elements and specifying them as a pattern for action. The fact that the resulting lists of specification are bathetic is rarely discussed by the international network of effectiveness researchers.

Instruction

The advent of the machine as a tool in classrooms and for administration had been foreseen from at least the 1920s. Skinner (1958) refers to machines designed by Pressey in the 1920s to test intelligence and recall. He describes the innovation:

In using the device the student refers to a numbered item in a multiple-choice test. He presses the button corresponding to his first choice of answer. If he is right, the device moves on to the next item; if he is wrong, the error is tallied, and he must continue to make choices until he is right . . . Such machines, Pressey pointed out . . . could not only test and score, they could *teach.* (p. 969, original emphasis)

The potential of the machine to teach continues to be vaunted, and its ever-increasing use predicted, repeating Skinner's 1950s prognostications. For example, Freidman (2000), in his article entitled *The Marvellous Medical Education Machine,* sees computers sweeping to the forefront in the race for progress and pushing aside all resistance.

The machine is coming; it is inevitable. It will gradually and by dint of great creative effort unstick medical education in space, time, and content. Those who ignore it run the risk of becoming irrelevant; those who embrace it can do enormous good. (p. 502)

Freidman's vision is of medical trainees who spend an increasing proportion of their time with computer simulations, rather than with actual patients. While there is no doubt advantage in training in this way, there is a smack of compulsion to embrace a system from which humans have been eliminated, where those who ignore the machine are irrelevant. Clegg (2001) characterizes such attitudes as widespread, and as pitching technophiliacs in opposition to pathological technophobes. She describes the US-military-dominated development of computers from the 1950s, which led to the increasing use of computers in schools from the 1970s. Their use is linked to "ideologies of the machine" (p. 308) and to "all American images of the industrial military complex" (p. 313). The embedding of the machine in education is therefore deeply gendered. Girls and women can, of course, relish the use of computers in their education as much as men. However, there is something of a masculine style that is negative in the line of prescriptions such as those of Skinner (1958) and Freidman (2000) and others (Woolgar, 2000). The ability of the computer to service the needs of the masses more cheaply than teachers face-to-face, and to function consistently without involving messy and expensive human involvement, are machine-like attributes increasingly and disturbingly embedded in our schools. Some may respond by dismissing such dystopian concerns as hysteria but, as Clegg (2001) reminds us, "the position of women as hysteric is, of course, a trope that has dominated much feminist thought" (p. 312). The machine metaphor demands that we do not dismiss such concern, but pull apart and analyze the features of education that are machine-like, and whether or not we can accept them with pleasure or equanimity.

Producing Identical Outputs

Leaders are adjured to match multiple sets of specifications, for themselves, their staff, and the curriculum and student attainment. They are also kept under surveillance to ensure compliance. Chapter 6 discusses in detail the degree to which the performative context ensures that leaders are monitored. Specification without compliance would not necessarily produce identical outputs, so systems to extort compliance are key. Taylor Fitz-Gibbon (1996) distinguishes performance and compliance indicators:

> A "performance indicator" can be defined as an item of information collected at regular intervals to track the performance of a system . . . Compliance indicators are checks as to whether some required features have been implemented. (p. 5)

This distinction is not discussed in UK schools, where generally the term used is "performance indicator." However, it is clear that sometimes the use of data is to encourage compliance. For example, guidance is provided to schools in England and Wales to help with self-evaluation (Department for Education and Skills, & Ofsted, 2006). The "guidance" makes clear the expectation that schools will use a national system of comparing data, the system called RAISEonline. This enables not just year-on-year internal comparison of results, but comparison with other schools in similar circumstances. Leaders are expected to embed scrutiny of comparative data as a frequent activity. Where performance is deemed unsatisfactory by inspectors, the school is put into special measures and change exacted. Although this is called self-evaluation, it looks remarkably like the use of compliance indicators.

In the US, the passage of Public Law 107–110, or No Child Left Behind (NCLB), is filled with requirements for creating uniformity and machine perfection and efficiency. By the year 2013–2014, all students are expected to attain certain minimum proficiencies or raise their attainment in reading and language, arts, and mathematics. All limited English-speaking students will become proficient in English. Highly qualified teachers will teach all students, and all students will graduate from high school. Since education in the US is the province of state government under the Constitution, the federal law requires all of the states to implement a single accountability system. There must be annual measurable objectives that identify a minimum percentage of students that must meet or exceed the proficiency level required for academic proficiency. Racial and ethnic minorities will not be allowed to lag behind the majority. NCLB requires that there must be at least 95% of each racial or ethnic minority attaining as well or better than the majority. All of these indicators are rolled into one single measure, AYP, or average yearly progress. The emphasis on uniformity and accountability also includes the provision that if schools consistently fail to make AYP they are labeled "unsafe," and local authorities must then notify parents and offer students an opportunity to transfer to another school while the "unsafe school" is required to create a corrective action plan, among other measures.

It is clear that the dominant metaphor here is the machine, because only machines have such consistently high levels of performance. Only machines have strict levels of uniformity that have very little deviance. And while the machine metaphor remains pervasive in the law, the mechanisms to eliminate deviation are strangely absent. The law requires actions to be performed, but is silent on how to deal with the large variances that exist in the human realm. It is a classic case of confusing "things of logic for the logic of things" (Bourdieu, 1998, p. 101). And the pervasive misapplication of the machine metaphor in thinking about the human realm amounts to a sort of "magical thinking," where stipulating something means it will somehow happen because it has been said.

EVALUATING THE MACHINE

Many of the outputs described in the discussion above, raising standards or equivalency in schools' performance, could be seen as admirable aims, and there is evidence that these aims have been achieved to some degree in the UK since the late twentieth century. In the US, the impact of NCLB has brought about some standardization of expectations, but huge problems remain, and it is unlikely that the levels of efficiency and uniformity specified in the law will be attained at all. Over time, it is likely that the efforts aimed at efficiency for all will be tempered with a bit more reality. It is doubtful that all students will attain any specific educational goal unless set very low, and there is a move to substitute "growth" toward a goal as an acceptable indicator of progress, instead of attainment of a uniform goal that everyone must meet. Clearly, the variable human contradicts the machine calculus. The machine metaphor, comparing an efficient machine to a school, evokes uneasiness. The virtues of machines may have been harnessed at a cost. If education's brief is narrowly pragmatic, to fit students for a productive place in the economy, then the focus on an efficient transmission of skills and knowledge as assessed by examination may be appropriate. If, however, we aspire to a wider vision of education as a means of supporting citizenship and the public good (Dewey, 1916/1966), or as a means of challenging oppression in a way that aims at more than getting the disadvantaged into "good" universities and jobs (Freire, 1996), then the mechanization of education may be counterproductive.

ON BEING A MACHINE

Acting with consistency and regularity is one aspect of a machine, and this chapter has explored the degree to which leaders must expect others to function in this way. The second defining attribute of machines is that they act without thought or emotion and without a guiding intelligence. The latter concept is variously understood, but might be assumed for our purposes to be apparent not only in the sophisticated synthesis of experience and many kinds of relevant data to make judgments, but in the integral place of emotion and of values in the process. How far leaders model values and emotional behavior and influence them in faculty and students is the exercise of intelligence that distinguishes man from machine and is the charter mark of leadership, which is humanist rather than mechanical.

Faculty themselves speak of the centrality in their work of both an emotional connection to learners and of the deeply felt wish to adjust learning to the needs of the individual (O'Connor, 2008); that is, they exercise high levels of responsive, intelligent judgment. Nowhere is this more intensely felt than in kindergarten or nursery and elementary or primary schools, where the development of very young children is at stake. The Plowden Report (Central Advisory Council for Education, 1967) was a landmark moment in the UK in the development of curriculum and pedagogy for children under eleven years of age. Plowden rejected an over-regularized system:

> There is little place for the type of scheme which sets down exactly what ground should be covered and what skill should be acquired by each class in the school. (para. 539)

The role of the teacher was emphasized to be adaptive to the child:

> The idea of flexibility has found expression in a number of practices, all of them designed to make good use of the interest and curiosity of children, to minimise the notion of subject matter being rigidly compartmental, and to allow the teacher to adopt a consultative, guiding, stimulating role rather than a purely didactic one. (para. 540)

The report explicitly rejected the utilitarian values of Gradgrind mentioned earlier. Instead, "the curriculum [was] to be thought of in terms of activity and experience rather than of knowledge to be acquired and facts to be stored" (Central Advisory Council for Education, 1967, para. 529), and Skinner's simplistic notions of mechanized learning, wherein

> Even simple segments of learning do not always conform closely to models of learning theory such as Skinner's. It is in a whole situation with a history behind it that a child or adult learns. (para. 519)

However, in the UK, revolt against what was seen as the liberal and inefficient education promoted by Plowden fueled decades of policy to assure quality and raise standards. Yet faculty still insist that the vision outlined in Plowden remains as relevant as ever (Forrester, 2005). In the US, the increasing resistance of teacher unions and many administrators to the huge increase in testing has created a backlash to such notions as "data-driven decision making," as Emery and Ohanian (2004) caution that the use of machines without a social conscience led to such past occurrences as when IBM data sorters were used to create the Auschwitz tattoo for the Third Reich (p. 13).

Given that the performance of leaders is shaped by the panoptic surveillance to which they are subject (see Chapter 6), the degree to which leaders model and encourage humanist values is difficult to discern. A study of high school education in England involving 45 schools (Gorard et al., 2009) found that principals and other leaders of schools repeatedly expressed their wish to focus on goals other than test results and to develop the whole student. They also believed that they were unable to do so because of perceived pressures. Many students felt their goals were funneled narrowly toward examinations. There is evidence that faculty feel the same pressure from principals and other leaders. In Jeffrey's study (2002) the destruction of positive relations between the senior management team and others is related strongly to the performative environment. A deputy principal recounts when, in preparing for inspection, she made a teacher cry,

> Tears came to her eyes, and I thought, "Oh God, I've done it again!" It's my management role, I've got no choice. I thought I was actually being quite helpful by photocopying some more check sheets and giving them to her when she arrived this morning. (p. 539)

The same deputy principal believed she had "become less sympathetic" (Jeffrey, 2002, p. 537). A second deputy believed teachers saw her as "somebody who checks up on your work" (p. 539), and a third that inspectors have "stripped the self" (p. 541). Individuality and sympathy make way for insistence on performance and compliance. Positive emotions are removed.

There is relatively little research on the emotional relationship of leaders and faculty in education. Bono, Foldes, Vinson, and Muros (2007), in reviewing studies of workplaces, suggest that leaders are likely to have a negative impact on the emotions of employees because they evaluate work and because they limit autonomy. While many interactions may be positive, those that are negative disproportionately impact an employee's mood and so motivation and tenor at work. If, as Bono and colleagues found, employees "experience less optimism, happiness, and enthusiasm when they interact with supervisors than when they interact with customers, clients, and coworkers" (p. 1363) then, in the hothouse context of schools, it would seem that leaders are likely to be sucking positive emotion from the environment. In a reduction of sympathy and a reduced willingness to accommodate the individual, they themselves have become machine-like and are contributing to the dehumanizing of schools.

THE MACHINE METAPHOR

The machine metaphor has led us through an exploration of how far schools and systems align to the factors that define machinery and mechanization and has raised some disturbing questions about the practice and direction of policy and leadership.

CONTEXT

Machines are thought of as the product of industrialized society and so a very recent influence on human history, giving rise to what Mintzberg (1983) has called the "machine bureaucracy," which is characterized by "standardization of work processes" (p. 23). Machine bureaucracies require stability in the environment, simple structures, and external control. In fact, as Mintzberg (1983) notes, "The implicit motto of the Machine Bureaucracy seems to be, 'When in doubt, control.' All problems are to be solved by the turning of the technocratic screws" (p. 180).

Considering the relevance of a machine metaphor to schooling and leaders has therefore demanded consideration of twentieth- and twenty-first-century angst about mechanization and computers. Less expectedly, it has also connected current policy to a much longer period of history. The implied values of machine-like schools and leaders resonate with attempts through many cultures and over many centuries to use education as a reductive utilitarian tool for the economy and for society. While many would argue that the emphasis on standards and on quality is designed to ensure that those who are disadvantaged are no longer left behind, our exploration of the machine metaphor leads us to consider a different motivation behind policy: a view of children and young people as raw materials destined for their economic role. Failures are industrial waste. For example, President George W. Bush (Office of the Press Secretary, 2004), in a speech to discuss education and the changing job market, compared failing children to a gap in the pipeline, a sort of factory escape of a valuable commodity. Goodwin (1996) suggests that how we use language frames how we see problems and solutions. The evidence assembled in this chapter suggests that policy makers are thinking of faculty and students in belittling ways, replacing early twentieth-century theory about how children learn and the full role education can play in the growth of human society with "one size fits all" control systems (Poletti, 2004). As a vision of humanity, it is as bleak as anything embodied in the dystopian works of art of the twentieth century depicting the use of dehumanized labor or robots, such as Orwell's (1945) novel *Animal Farm* or Ridley Scott's 1982 film *Blade Runner*.

LEADERSHIP PRACTICE

If language shapes thought, the metaphors in educational discourse indicate how leaders think and function. We "deliver" not learning, but "provision" to our "intake." These have become dead metaphors. We no longer think what is implied by the metaphoric comparison. Educational leaders may strive to act in ways that are learner centered and transformational, but ubiquitous machine metaphors suggest that they are fighting a battle that is often not won.

LEADERSHIP DEVELOPMENT NEEDS

We have argued elsewhere (Lumby & English, 2009) that leaders' development needs to be primarily focused on deepening awareness of their identities, rather than on acquiring techniques influenced by competencies and standards. This chapter strengthens that argument. There is no simple prescription to resist the mechanizing pressures of education policy in many parts of the world, but awareness of the deeper implications, of what is implied about children and about society and the relationship between to the two, is a proper core issue for leadership preparation programs. There is some evidence that leaders want to engage with what they see as the important stuff; that is the core elements of measuring and raising school performance through sets of standards and competencies, and resist what some see as diversions into political issues (Rusch, 2004). Education has always been the crucible where the elements of humanity are shaped. If the dehumanizing propensity of current policy and practice is to be resisted, then the important stuff is not learning about how to raise standards or assure quality, but how to wholeheartedly maintain the guiding intelligence of creative and empathetic leaders of schools.

The machine metaphor is seductive and simple. Its simplicity both masks and miniaturizes the complexities to which it is applied. Its success rests on a closed system of logic where inputs, throughputs, and outputs can be meshed with measures of efficiency. And, as Usher and Edwards (1994) have cogently observed, efficiency is basically a teleology because it has no end; it is the end. It is completely self-contained and is its own justification (p. 166). Machines have no moral purposes, values, dreams, or feelings. To make their virtues the goals of education is, in the end, dehumanizing for, as Mintzberg (1983) has observed, treating people as categories rather than as individuals has the "consequence of destroying the meaning of work itself" (p. 178). To treat children as educable units by consistent repetitive means jeopardizes not only their individual potential but our future as a humane society.

3

Leadership as Accounting

. . . the world has gone quantitative, and statistics sell as well as, if not better than, anecdotes—provided one wins the race to place one's preferred numbers in the preferred media.

—Adelman (2006, p. B7)

As a word, "accountability" is a concept, an adjective, and a world-view. It is omniscient in contemporary educational contexts. It has simultaneously become the problem and the solution to worldwide educational issues; that is, the reason schools are not improving is because they are not accountable, and the solution is to make them accountable. In the US, this problem/antidote/rhetorical legerdemain was squarely behind the 2009 "new" Obama educational plan called "Race to the Top" (Ready, Set, Go: Reviving America's Schools, 2009), which was really the same old race, in the same old place, with the same old face.

What educational leaders and policy wonks often fail to understand is that the accounting metaphor, so easily applied to schools, comes with enormous academic and popular corporate baggage. And while in the UK and the US it is a near-universal password for what is wrong with schools and how they need to be reformed and transformed, it is a context-embedded idea with a long history of shortcomings in both the public and private sectors. Despite the failures of the "accountability" concept, it has become a truism no longer even contested; in short, a metanarrative, where it is viewed as always truthful and few even bother to think about seriously challenging its supremacy, even though it may not be true at all (see Cherryholmes, 1988, p. 11). In the process, what has been a public service for the common good becomes another venue for making money. Schemes for profit making and enhancement in the corporate world, such as voucher plans and other forms of privatization, are advanced as solutions to "our failing public schools" (Emery & Ohanian, 2004, p. 6). In short, we have a defense for the slogan reaching back to Adam Smith in 1776, that "greed is good" (Black, 2006, p. 29). In the last thirty years, the "accountability movement" has attained a near-complete transcendence in the language of educational policy and how problems are conceived and resolved in education (see Lindle & Cibulka, 2006). Hopmann (2008) asks, "What makes (some) governments tremble, parliaments discuss, journalists write, parents nervous, and teachers angry?" (p. 417). The answer is the international bookkeeping of education, the *Programme for International Student Assessment* (*PISA*), a triennial international test of 15-year-old school children's performance. The results have the power to cause panic at the highest government levels.

Accounting and its derivative term, "accountability," have come to signify the following when describing educational leadership:

- The relentless drive to quantify and subsequently measure all aspects of the schooling process
- The quest to connect what is measured as outputs to what is involved with securing the resources to attain them, that is, inputs, forming a tight connection of means to ends, thus enabling strategies of cost reduction and application of efficiency measures and the idea of "value added" to educational operations (Odden & Picus, 2004, p. 126; Hanushek, 1997; Kupermintz, 2003)
- The linkage of administrative and teaching actions and tasks to the attainment of desired and predicted student outcomes, principally as stipulated in test scores on selected curriculum content, creating a measurement base to support the concept of "best practices," or, what is "best" produces the highest test scores (see Levačić & Glatter, 2001; Karp, 2002). This concept forms the idea of "no nonsense" educational leadership and is responsible in part for the movement to bring in outsiders to educational leadership positions in some US school systems, called by Eisinger and Hula (2004) "gunslinger superintendents" (p. 621).
- The portrayal of excellent or outstanding education as quantified to form a base of comparison, evaluation, and judgment about which schools, school leaders, and teachers are "the best" at what they do, with calls for paying these "outstanding practitioners" more than the rest, based on their test score results

ℯ The elimination of all that is "subjective" about the educational process unless it can be measured and quantified, that is, the complete rationalization of all education into league tables, bar graphs, and pie charts for easy public consumption and media portrayals and manipulation, with subsequent editorial calls to eliminate poor schools as wasteful, squandering the national wealth of the human resource gene pool, and placing the nation at a competitive disadvantage in the global race for corporate profits and national wealth, prestige, military and political prowess, and dominance over other nations

ℯ The reduction of leadership preparation to the essential skills to produce high-performing schools, as defined by high test scores on selected curriculum content

As we explore the ramifications of the accounting metaphor and its hegemony over educational leadership, we should be reminded of the warning by Adelman (2006):

> You are participants in a dynamic landscape of persuasion in a democratic society. Look carefully across the landscape and you will see parties asserting influence through the selection and/or manipulation of symbols. . . . Those purveyors of unofficial data create a limited field of vision, from which follow policies with unintended, unpleasing, or irrelevant consequences. (p. B9)

THE RELENTLESS PURSUIT OF RATIONALITY AND WASTE

Rationality is a key ingredient of bureaucratic and corporate life. Weber (1946/1970) spoke of the objectivity of the bureaucracy as one of its defining features and noted that such objectivity was an arbitrary ingredient. He supported the idea of "reasons of the state . . . as the supreme and ultimate guiding star of the official's behavior" (p. 220). He also added:

> The only decisive point for us is that in principle a system of rationally debatable "reasons" stands behind every act of bureaucratic administration, that is, either subsumption under norms or a weighing of ends and means. (p. 220)

Weber's prescient analysis reveals that bureaucratic and corporate rationality is a social construct and not a natural phenomenon. As such, it rests on certain "debatable reasons," or claims and assumptions. Whatever the manifestation, when examining forms of accountability, these must be considered in context. It is not simply "accounting," but "accountability," that comes with an apparatus (a construct connecting means and ends together) that is political, economic, and social in its applications. As Weber (1946/1970) notes: "The bureaucratic structure goes hand in hand with the concentration of the material means of management in the hands of the master" (p. 221). It is this propensity of bureaucratic and corporate existence that gives accountability schemes as advanced by corporate moguls from a "for-profit" perspective their antidemocratic persuasion. The people are not to be asked. They are to be told.

The implementation of any accountability scheme or derivative requires not simply clear cut goals that are quantifiable and measurable, but a complete "managing-for-results" system. Watson (1981) has described this system by indicating that it should be comprised of the following components:

1. Results-oriented thinking

2. Ability to prepare goals

3. Good organization

4. Good communication flows about mission, objectives, and policies

5. Goal setting

6. Goals selected for effectiveness and vitality

7. Well-devised plans

8. Goal reviews

9. Developmental leadership

10. Performance evaluation

11. Employee development, and

12. System reviews and audits (pp. 68–70)

Watson's description is echoed by what Michael Fullan (2009) has called "whole-system reform" where "leadership development . . . is a means to an end, combining job-embedded, organization-embedded, and system-embedded reform . . ." (p. 48). Watson (1981) suggested that such an approach means adopting a total mindset about visualizing how to manage anything, from making toothpaste to teaching. The "bottom line," a term with a clear accounting linkage, is the adoption of "commonsense business management practices that every company must use, from the corner drug store on up to General Motors" (Grace, 1984, p. 5). This is the most overt statement from a business executive, J. Peter Grace, chairman of former President Reagan's Private Sector Survey on Cost Control, that a for-profit, accounting or economic model is appropriate as a mental construct to impose on public sector services, government, and education.

This transfer from one sector to the other is based on assumptions that are highly questionable, among them that such forms of rationality are appropriate for education, and that the function of leadership is to reduce waste and maximize output. The statement is also ironic, as General Motors has since gone "belly-up" as a corporation. The final moment came when President Barack Obama's Automotive Task Force demanded that General Motors' CEO, Rick Wagoner, be removed as a key to recovery at the former auto giant (Ingrassia, 2009). Maryann Keller (1989) in her book, *Rude Awakening*, had warned:

> As long as the unwritten rule stands that the best way to achieve success at GM is to be a good finance man, the bad habit of juggling numbers in order to present the picture people *want* to see cannot be broken. This is one of the most deeply ingrained cultural problems at General Motors. (emphasis in the original, p. 253)

Paul Ingrassia (2009) summarized Detroit's historic plunge from market dominance to industrial ragamuffin when he observed, "In all of this lies a tale of hubris, missed opportunities, disastrous decisions, and flawed leadership of almost biblical proportions" (p. A21).

This was especially true with General Motors' infatuation with "a manipulation of numbers," (Keller, 1989, p. 254) in which "GM ended up investing in million-dollar solutions for ten-cent problems—instead of finding ten-cent solutions for million-dollar problems" (p. 205).

The worship of numbers and accounting ledgers is one of the hallmarks of capitalism, according to Max Weber (1946/1970). Weber indicated that a linkage between rationality and bookkeeping was the heart of capitalism and that this practice contained a methodical, rational way of life and became an avenue of "proving oneself before God in the sense of attaining salvation" (p. 321). Schumpeter (1942/1950) opined that capitalism "turns the unit of money into a tool of rational cost-profit calculations, of which the towering monument is double-entry bookkeeping" (p. 123). Indeed, in his biography of John D. Rockefeller, Chernow (1998) observes that the richest man in America in his time began his life as a bookkeeper when, he said later, he "learned to have great respect for figures and facts, no matter how small they were . . . [he] had a passion for detail which afterward [he] was forced to strive to modify" (p. 46). Rockefeller's business ethics became the relentless pursuit of profit, employing every practice possible to shut down his competition and attain monopoly over oil refining. This clear-cut goal was pursued by tactics that included fear, intimidation, and bribery of public officials among other coercive and tawdry tactics. Rockefeller had no ethics when it came to his goal of dominance in oil. Ethics are not about numbers or accountability but about values, and they are not reducible to the logos of rationalism and mathematical analysis.

When former business executives prognosticate about how to "fix" educational problems, the for-profit mindset becomes prominent. For example, former IBM CEO Lou Gerstner, Jr., and author of *Who Says Elephants Can't Dance?* (2002), indicates that the secret of success is not to confuse vision with steely-eyed strategies that are initiated with "massive amounts of quantitative analysis" (p. 223). This will lead to asking hard questions and to maintaining a strategic focus. As for how to "fix" schools, here is Gerstner's "vision":

> We need high, rigorous standards, we need great teachers supported by high compensation for the very best teachers. We need more time on task, we need a longer school day, we need a longer school year, and we need accountability and measurement in the system so we can constantly adjust what's going on. That's it, it's all we need. So, the problem isn't that we don't know what to do. ("Failing Our Children," 2008, p. R9)

As for Gerstner's solution, the first thing he would do is abolish all 16,000 school districts in the US ("Failing Our Children," 2008). His rationale for this move is that

> . . . when I took over IBM I found I had 81 profit centers. Oh my God: How am I going to create change with 81 profit centers? How'd you like to create change with 16,000 profit centers? These organizations stand in the way of what we want to do. ("Failing Our Children," 2008, p. R9)

Although the corporate accountability movement in education takes on the tone of a religious crusade, the imposition of the corporate accountability model is profoundly antidemocratic. It is antidemocratic in that the concept of local school governance as embodied in school districts permits variance from a standardized curriculum and standardized tests. School districts with their own governance systems might not embrace such standards or such measures. They might see a different "vision" to what Gerstner, or other corporate mavens, sees. But there is in Gerstner and others a definite top-down mentality to accountability, which is the environment in which corporations function. They are not democracies, and their tactics are about maximizing profits. There is little, if anything, in them regarding providing public services that benefit the larger society or services that are too expensive.

Larry Cuban (2004) has chronicled other corporate influences on schools. Superintendents are now called CEOs, and curriculum directors are "chief academic officers." Superintendents now have their salaries tied to student performance improvement as represented in test score gains; despite the fact that many CEOs are not paid on the basis of their organization's performance, and many that are receive huge bonuses when their organizations perform poorly. For example, Ara Hovnanian's home-building business experienced a stock loss of 62%, a 31% decrease in revenue, and the company lost $1.1 billion, but Mr. Hovnanian received a bonus of $1.5 million. Edgar Bronfman Jr., CEO of Warner Music Group, similarly oversaw his company's $56 million dollar net income loss and a 25% decrease in stock value, but received a $3 million dollar bonus. The educational equivalent is the very high salaries paid to principals, whatever their school's results. In Yorkshire, England, in 2009 the average salary of a secondary school head teacher in the city of Leeds was almost £85,000. One "super head" was being paid £126,000 (Robinson, 2009). This salary was reported as more than five times the average Yorkshire wage of approximately £23,000. Similar instances are reported throughout England, with some principals earning more than the Minister for Education. Others earn twice the average salary as consultancy fees to "failing" schools, in addition to their regular salary. A deal is struck with Governing Boards allowing the principal to generate fees that are shared with the school (Marley & Judd, 2009). It is a lucrative business; £50,000 per annum is reported as a typical sum. The ever-rising salaries follow the pattern of those of corporate leaders. The Minister for Education in the UK announced in 2009 that super heads who turned struggling schools into academies (which involves corporate sponsorship) or those who run chains of schools will be paid £200,000 per annum (Ross, 2009). The language used of chains, branding, and executive leaders render schools unrecognizable as community services.

But, as Cuban (2004) notes, the language of business and its notions of accountability are liberally sprinkled throughout educational administration with terms like "continuous improvement," "benchmarking," "customer satisfaction," and "total quality management." We find these and other terms embedded in the ISLLC (Interstate Leaders Licensure Consortium) standards for school administrators in the US (see Shipman, Queen, & Peel, 2007), such as changing school culture (p. 10); chief financial officer (p. 61); data analysis and collection (pp. 4–5); human resource management (p. 60); instructional standards (pp. 27–54); vision statements (pp. 112–113); visionary leadership (pp. 17–18); learning best practices (p. 38); marketing strategies (p. 94); media commandments (p. 7); message enhancers (p. 7); mission statements (p. 14); Planning, Programming Budgeting System (PPBS) (pp. 68–69); data-driven reform (pp. 4–5); site-based management (p. 22); systems theory (p. 4); value-added leadership (p. 127); strategic planning (p. 3); and zero tolerance (p. 77). Similarly, in the UK, the National Standards for Headteachers (DfES, 2004) refer to "securing accountability" (p. 10) by performance management and quality assurance systems.

Such terms demonstrate that "accountability" is more than simple "accounting," that is, bookkeeping. Accountability is an ideology, and as an ideology it assumes a status that is considerably more powerful and pervasive. Even a cursory review of these standards reinforces Weber's (1946/1970) belief that bureaucracy tightens the power and control of "the master" (p. 221). There is nothing in such standards that loosens the hold of the single school administrator as the one person who is indispensable in successful implementation of "accountability." It also explains why some former business CEOs, such as Eli Broad, a billionaire who spends millions trying to "reform" schools in the US by hiring noneducators with business degrees or military backgrounds, despises schools of education, teacher unions, and school boards (Riley, 2009; Weinberg, 2003). This is virtually the same view held by former IBM CEO Louis Gerstner. According to these private sector leaders, what the schools need in order to be improved are new "masters" running them. And "accountability" is about corporatizing schools within tighter means-ends connections, ruthless cost reduction strategies to deal with waste, and tons of testing to measure "results" and weed out incompetent teachers and administrators. According to some business moguls, all that schools of education, school boards, and teacher unions want to do is to maintain the status quo.

What these same leaders fail to realize is that the "accountability" model they advocate embraces the status quo, because it has vastly oversimplified the nature of the problem and leaves the complicated issues of teaching and learning untouched. Cuban (2004) observes,

> What business-inspired reformers wanted for state and local curricula, tests, and "bottom line" accountability has largely been achieved at the cost of preserving orthodox school organization and conventional teaching practices that an earlier generation of business-led reformers severely criticized as both traditional and regimented. (p. 111)

The reasons why the current model of "accountability" will not improve all of the schools has been stipulated by Arthur Wise (1979) in his book, *Legislated Learning: The Bureaucratization of the American Classroom*. It involves attributing to the "accountability" ideology a good deal of wishful thinking called, by Wise, "hyperrationalization."

EDUCATIONAL HYPERRATIONALIZATION

Rationality in bureaucratic life generally refers to how an individual leader engages in rendering positional situated decisions within a role and a hierarchy. Viewed from the dominant perspective in which such acts are described and researched today, and within what Bourdieu (2001) has called an epistemocratic justification, decisions are embedded in normative decision theory that postulates that, when leaders render a decision, they can make it independently of others and that it may be divided into two parts: an objective and subjective section. The objective part is organized by formal rules that involve selecting among alternatives "using elimination procedures, ranking procedures, and sometimes even optimization procedures" (Clough, 1984, p. 23). Such analytical methods depend on accepted standard measures "of performance and value . . ."

and they "depend heavily on socially accepted threshold limits for the elimination of alternatives" (Clough, 1984, p. 23). Making such approaches "routine" is centered in "the logical structuring of comparisons" (Clough, 1984, p. 23). Subjectivity of a decision is thought to rest in values related to personal utility or Simon's (1945) "economic man," where motives are reduced to an economic theory of exchange. In this presentation of decision making there is no place for emotion, intuition, or anything that is not calculable, predictable, and controllable (see Bolton & English, 2009).

It should be clear that, for rationality to exist in an organization, both its external and internal environments have to become stabilized and routinized. Forces that are not controllable must be tamed, if not outright, by direct managerial control, through hierarchical hegemony, then by statistical assumptions or epistemocratic justifications. Unpredictability in all forms must be eliminated or severely reduced. Democracy is, of course, unpredictable at times. To corporate heads, the necessary condition for comparisons of alternatives is centered on the reduction of uncertainty. Rationality requires the ruthless elimination of uncertainty, so the adoption of the ideology of "accountability" means reshaping an entire human organization so that it conforms to normative and rule-based behaviors. More than anything else, corporate analytical models rest on cost-effective preferences that are supported by assumptions of rationality, consistency, and stability. The peaks and valleys of human learning curves must be flattened out and made manageable. Teaching must be routinized because concepts of test reliability (the basis of comparisons) rest on standardization of both teaching and learning. This is one reason why advocates of "accountability" from the corporate sector are silent about matters of teaching and learning. But it is the reason why such "reforms" miss "the process of education—how educational practice actually affects the child. The practice of education is thus to be altered without an understanding of how education occurs" (Wise, 1979, p. 56).

Whatever the sources of variance leading to unpredictability, they are sources of uncertainty and so threats to the agendas of those who are in charge. Teacher unions and school boards just don't figure to be controllable and so must be eliminated or their power constrained. And schools of education that prepare educational leaders must be eradicated because graduates from these sites ask too many questions and are skeptical of the motivation and outcomes of the kind of system advocated as good for schools from a for-profit perspective (see House, 1998; Saltman, 2000).

The concept of hyperrationalization refers to a process that increases the bureaucratic overlay of the schools "without attaining the intended policy objectives" (Wise, 1979, pp. 47–48). Thus, hyperrationalization represents an extension in the assumed locus of rationality embedded in the ideology of "accountability," which is not justified or possible. In short, the necessity for stability and predictability required by "accountability" models exceeds what is actually possible in schools and school systems. It is this fact that escapes the corporate reformers. It isn't that educators didn't believe in their ideology; it is rather that it has been fully tried and has failed, producing what Gerstner (2008) has called "forty years of failed school reform" (p. A9). It is unlikely that President Obama's 2009 "Race to the Top" is any different than all the other failed reforms, as it was ensconced in the same "accountability" 'framework, with the same assumptions. Wise (1979) has indicated that the theory of education that underlies much reform, and we would add is evident in the "Race to the Top," is that children are pliable and come to school willing to be molded and shaped by them; teachers are similarly pliable and will go along with the expectations and exert maximum effort to implement the law as intended; that there is a science of education that will produce a standard-ized response as a form of equal treatments that can then be rationally assessed with the extant measurement tools available; and, finally, that administrators and teachers will always prefer cost-effective responses over those that are not as cost-effective (p. 57). All of these assumptions rest on a tight relationship between means and ends in schools. However, as Wise (1979) points out, "the problem with scientific rationality is that its conditions can almost never be satisfied in everyday educational settings" (p. 70). And what happens when the requirements of the policy planners exceed the reality in the schools? One result is what Callahan (2004) has called "the cheating culture."

THE CHEATING CULTURE: CORROSION OF THE MEANS/ENDS ACCOUNTABILITY CONTINUUM

The evidence that hyperrationalization is at work in education has emerged. For example, franchising arrangements in the UK, that is, licens-ing courses to other organizations and taking a fee for doing so, has led to numerous cases of alleged financial impropriety by principals of colleges and universities from the 1990s, where academic standards are relaxed to allow a lucrative business to proceed. Schools and colleges are also recipi-ents of dubious sponsorship deals (Slater, 2003). However, such corruption has been present in the corporate sector for decades. We distinguish here the presence of out-and-out crooks such as Bernard Madoff (Frank & Efrati, 2009), who ran the largest known Ponzi scheme in history, from oth-erwise so-called "normal" people who, because of their circumstances, resort to cutting corners to comply with unreasonable job expectations.

Toffler (2003) quotes Arthur Levitt Jr., the former chairman of the Securities and Exchange Commission, as observing the following:

> Too many corporate managers, auditors, and analysts are participants in a game of nods and winks. In the zeal to satisfy consensus earnings estimates and project a smooth earnings path, wishful thinking may be winning the day over faithful representation. (p. 243)

Indeed, Toffler (2003) also reminds us that it isn't just a few "bad seeds" that have been spotted in the financial debacles since Enron that have caused a worldwide recession; rather, it is that "a great deal of wrong-doing in American business is the result of systemic problems" (p. 229). She describes it as " . . . ingrained cultural practices—pressure to meet targets, implicit ways of dealing with clients, information and how it is used—shape the behavior of more and more employees" (p. 229). In short, what she is describing is the "accountability" ideology in its most rampant form, in a mad chase for profits that involves shady accounting practices and outright cheating. In England, in a landmark national report, the further education sector was lambasted for running colleges as businesses to the detriment of disadvantaged students (Kennedy, 1997). The government reined the sector in, but Pandora's box was opened and would not be shut. Since the 1990s, UK schools, colleges, and universities are widely led not in a business-like way, but as if they were commercial businesses (Lumby & Morrison, 2006).

The posture of corporate culture that led to what Frank Partnoy (2003), in the title of his book, has called "infectious greed" was also identified by Callahan (2004) as a systemic issue when he observed, "The malaise besetting corporate America during the downturn of the decade led to the rise of a new breed of corporate leaders and money managers who called for a take-no-prisoners brand of the bottom line of business" (p. 44). Notes Callahan (2004), it wasn't about just survival; "it was about increasing efficiency and, ultimately, profits" (p. 44).

What encouraged the cheating culture was the practice of connecting executive pay to the "performance expectations" of a company's stock on Wall Street. This "pay for performance" has been advocated for teachers and school leaders over a long time period and was embedded in President Obama's "Race to the Top" manifesto (Meckler, 2009).

Other financial practices that inflate company revenue and that were connected to CEO pay have involved outright fraud. For example, Dell Inc., the computer company, had to restate its earnings by $50 million because of "improper adjustments to various reserve and accrued-liability accounts on the balance sheet—usually at the close of the quarter to give the appearance that quarterly goals were met" (Lawton & Clark, 2007, p. A3). The scandal resulted in the resignation of the CEO and the chief financial officer of the company. General Electric Company, one of America's blue chip corporations, had to pay a $50 million dollar fine for misstating its revenue for two years, which resulted in over-stipulating its income by $200 million. As quoted in Glader and Scannell, "had it not changed the methodology [of the overstatement] the commission said, GE would have missed analysts' earnings estimates for the first time in eight years" (2009, p. B2). Robert Khuzami, director of the SEC's Division of Enforcement, observed, "GE bent the accounting rules beyond the breaking point" (Glader & Scannell, 2009, p. B2).

Clearly, these incidents and indictments are illustrative of the culture of abuse within the dominant "accountability" model in the private sector, the same model that is advocated by business CEOs for public education (Bersin, 2005). The wide range of abuses, the incentives to cheat based on pressures to reach preassigned targets, a culture of so-called "no-nonsense" and "no excuses" expectations, and the connection of CEO tenure to earnings projections and stock prices, have led to a pervasive cheating culture the likes of which so far have not been prevalent in education. There is evidence that it is beginning to emerge, with the increased emphasis on test scores; for example, in DeKalb County, Georgia, two school administrators were suspended from their positions after they were involved in changing students' answers on fifth-grade math tests. The scandal also involved eight other educators in three other elementary schools. The two school administrators were also charged in a criminal offense because they falsified a state document, a penalty that involves a two- to ten-year prison term (Torres, 2009, p. A1).

In England in 2009, the House of Commons Education Select Committee investigated the alleged rise in cases of cheating by schools in Standard Attainment Tests. Such cheating was attributed to the pressure of maintaining a position in the league tables.

Not only does the evidence not support whole-school reform accountability models as a means for improving school achievement for all children (see Gross, Booker, & Goldhaber, 2009), but the plunge in public confidence based on the widespread corruption of business CEOs has resulted in a loss of faith in business leadership. In a list of occupations in the Harvard University's Center for Public Leadership survey, business leadership was ranked eighth in a field of eleven, only ahead of federal government leadership and the press. Educational leadership was ranked fourth. The Harvard survey found, "Eighty-three per cent of Americans say corporate leaders are more concerned with the bottom line than with running their companies well" (Brush, 2006, p. 36).

This public judgment should make educational leaders stop and seriously pause before embracing the sorts of easy and simple solutions being advanced at the present time, which are supposed to solve all the problems in providing all children with a quality education using an accounting metaphor for school leadership.

THE ACCOUNTING METAPHOR: A CHIMERA WRAPPED UP AS AN IDEOLOGY

CONTEXT

In ancient Greek mythology a *chimera* was a female monster with disparate parts—a lion's head, a goat's body, and a serpent's tail. But it also refers to "an illusion or fabrication of the mind, especially an unrealizable dream"

(Webster, 1971, p. 144). The "accountability" model embedded in nearly all school reform legislation is such an unrealizable dream. It has been applied across the board over several decades and failed to produce the results its advocates expound as its virtues.

The unrealizable dream is an ideology that Canguilheim (1988) defines as "reassuring fables, unconsciously complicit in a judgment determined by self-interest" (p. 31). An ideology is a kind of narrative or "a theory that cannot be debated, attacked, criticized, and ultimately exposed on its most basic premises and assumptions . . . Ideologies often rest on 'self-evident' or 'unexamined' truths" (English, 1994, p. 49). While accounting is a recognized technical process of determining the value of things, "accountability" is a master narrative that goes far beyond the process of accounting. It includes assumptions and practices that, when applied to complex processes and organizations, fail to produce the anticipated results; and more than anything else accountability, like accounting, is susceptible to human error, greed, and deception. This is even more so when the pressure is applied to produce unattainable results or, as Thomas O'Boyle (1988) wrote of the predatory culture installed at General Electric by Jack Welch:

> The bottom line is always that you had better make your bottom line. The constant pressure to "go get the numbers" has led, inevitably, to aberrant behavior. The impact this Darwinian mentality has had on General Electric is huge; the impact is [it] had on America is more complex. (p. 16)

The "accountability" model in business and education has largely gone uncriticized and unexamined. Its appeal to common sense and simple logic, as well as the zeal by which its proponents engage in advocacy and even prophecy about its power, have positioned it as an icon to be reckoned with, from the policy to the operational levels. Yet, there is abundant evidence that it has eroded the time-honored values of business life, which O'Boyle (1988) has identified as "loyalty, trust, respect, teamwork, hard work, compassion," and which have been thrown overboard "in a feverish pursuit of the quick buck" (p. 17).

LEADERSHIP PRACTICE

This chapter has put the spotlight on the "accounting metaphor" as a misguided effort to create a rational base to pursue profit, minimize waste, and attain impossible goals. When applied in the business world, it resulted in a stimulus for across-the-board cheating, deception, and fraud, and not just in a few isolated instances, a few bad apples, but numerous operators who behaved as crooks. However, while there were some who had always been criminal in their hearts, the vast majority were believed, by those who knew them, to be interested in doing good things and the right things, at least in the beginning. They did not begin as rule-benders but, when subjected to what Korten (2001) termed "corporate cannibalism" (p. 207), ordinary people learned to bend and then break the rules (O'Boyle, 1998).

We think that the leadership practices of corporate America are not appropriate for effective public service institutions and agencies that are not organized for profit, but to provide services to a designated range of clients. In defending these institutions, we are in the same position as Pierre Bourdieu (2001), who indicated that such a situation was paradoxical because " . . . one is led to defend programs or institutions that one wishes in any case to change, such as public services and the national state, which no one could rightly want to preserve as is, or unions or even public schooling, which must be continually subjected to the most merciless critique" (p. 23).

We believe that skills-based leadership programs anchored in the "accountability" mindset will not liberate schools or usher in radical new reforms, eliminate the achievement gap, solve the teacher shortage problem, prompt a decline in unemployment, or enhance international competitiveness of the nation state; all are agendas wrapped in the "accountability" logos.

The advocates of "accountability" have never acknowledged its limitations, that is, what it won't or can't do. Instead, the "accountability" model is advanced as a universal antidote to whatever ails business and educational systems, despite myriad failures that continually point back to it as a form of magical thinking. We believe that a sound critique of the limitations inherent in the "accountability" model should be part of leadership preparation and practice. Future school leaders must come to some fundamental understanding of the shortcomings of the complete "accountability" package in order to know where it may offer advantages and where it offers none.

LEADERSHIP DEVELOPMENT NEEDS

Above all, we believe that the story of "accountability" must be deconstructed so that leaders once again see that they have a responsibility to those with whom they work. Subordinates are not there to be manipulated, frightened, or goaded. Leaders' responsibilities begin with the most basic premise of all, that people matter more than outcomes and, while "profits are important . . . they must be measured in terms of their social consequences" (O'Boyle, 1998, p. 365). As long ago as 1986, Morgan warned of "the assault of rationalism on the human spirit" (p. 20) in organizational management. If accountability in its simplest definition means the obligation to give an account, then educators must account to current and future generations for the transmission of what upholds the human spirit and bear primary responsibility for that.

For now, we think the comment by Essig and Owens (2009) is *apropos* of the widespread use of the accounting metaphor in education: "Politics is the art of looking for trouble, finding it everywhere, diagnosing it incorrectly, and applying the wrong remedies" (p. B5).

4

Leadership as War

A good general, a well-organized system, good instruction, and severe discipline, aided by effective establishments, will always make good troops, independently of the cause for which they fight.

—Chandler (1987, p. 74)

Military commanders have served as beacons for those trying to understand leadership through time. Human history is littered with the battlefield exploits of victors and vanquished since Homer described the feats of Achilles in the Trojan War. There is something ultimate about war, because death is always imminent and is final. Mistakes are often fatal. Courage is visible. The outcome of a battle is clear. One army is beaten: the other army is victorious. The sheer violence and display of force leaves an indelible impression on the minds and emotions of those present. The great US Confederate General Robert E. Lee, acknowledging the seductive power of war, once remarked, "It is well that war is so terrible, or we should grow too fond of it" (quoted in Lawless, 1991, p. 62).

War also elevates some human characteristics over others that are admired. For example, when describing a true revolutionary leader, the legendary Che Guevara wrote the following:

> . . . the true revolutionary is guided by strong feelings of love. It is impossible to think of an authentic revolutionary without this

quality. This is perhaps one of the greatest dramas of a leader; he must combine an impassioned spirit with a cold mind and make painful decisions without flinching one muscle. (Anderson, 1997, p. 636)

Love is invoked as a justification for qualities of ruthlessness and single-mindedness, and for submerging emotion. The context of war makes admirable those qualities that might in peacetimes appear the contrary. The "cold mind" celebrated by Che Guevara requires a willingness to dehumanize others as the enemy and regard one's own as expendable; outside war, such attitudes might be despised. The crucible of war is stark and unambiguous for those who are the warriors. The brutality of war strips away discussion and niceties regarding leadership, and registers what is important in stark hues. What is important becomes a single goal—winning—as the ambiguities of messy life are peeled away.

It is this situational clarity that is appealing to leaders or potential leaders in other fields, including educators and their critics. In transposing the characteristics of the warrior to the institutional or educational agency leader, the code of the warrior and the landscape of battle offer a host of metaphors including such as "the culture wars" or the "math wars," where there are two opposing sides that are strongly entrenched.

Perhaps one of the most obvious documents in the US in which war metaphors are displayed prominently is the 1983 report called *A Nation at Risk*, issued by the US Department of Education's National Commission on Excellence in Education. This document painted a picture of a disorganized and dispirited system of schools and lackluster leaders and warned,

> If an unfriendly foreign power had attempted to impose on America the mediocre educational performance that exists today, we might well have viewed it as an act of war. As it stands, we have allowed this to happen to ourselves. We have even squandered the gains in student achievement made in the wake of the Sputnik challenge. Moreover, we have dismantled essential support systems which helped make those gains possible. We have, in effect, been committing an act of unthinking, unilateral educational disarmament. (p. 5)

The metaphors were designed to be shocking and they made headlines all over the country. Editorials appeared in most major newspapers and the national television networks featured the report (Bell, 1988, p. 131). The war images of a weakened nation disarming itself in the face of the threat of international competition for the world's resources, which would undermine "American prosperity, security, and civility" (p. 5), reverberated across the centuries as far back as Sun Tzu's dictum of the third or fifth century BCE, that " . . . a nation destroyed cannot be restored to existence, and the dead cannot be restored to life" (Sun Tzu, 1988, p. 26).

The utilization of the "crisis" metaphor has since become commonplace among educational critics from both the left and the right. Creating a "crisis" has become tantamount to then proffering the preferred solution to resolve it. It reflects an American proclivity to see war not as an extension of politics but "as crusades to punish evil" (Summers, 1982, p. 88). The *Nation at Risk* report amounted to a crusade to resolve long-standing educational problems in the US. In the main it was a failure because the "enemy" was not even characterized correctly.

The continued use of military metaphors was also marked in 2003 in the US with the release of The Broad Foundation and Thomas B. Fordham Institute's *Better Leaders for Better Schools.* Drawing on the familiar idea of creating a "crisis" in leadership, this anonymous attack on educational leadership was replete with military metaphors exclaiming that school superintendents were "education's field marshals" (p. 13). Military language is also embedded in education talk in the UK. For example, scanning the website of the National College for School Leadership (NCSL), Mongon and Chapman's (2008) report on successful leadership for white working-class learners refers to a practice where, "The team meets on a Thursday afternoon and goes through a list of 'target' students who have been identified as 'at risk' or 'missing'" (p. 17). The metaphor converts students into soldiers who are under threat or missing in action. Training material for principals on how to manage exclusion hearings refers to "the incursion" of a parent (Information for School and College Governors, 2004). On the website for the Department of Children Schools and Families (DCSF), the Chief Executive of the e-Learning Foundation describes "what will be a long battle to win the resources we need . . . a battle we joined in 2001 when we started" (Thompson, n.d.).

War has become an ubiquitous source of metaphors in the educational terrain. Some practitioners may be skeptical of this idea; their repulsion for war in the abstract leads them to believe that they do not themselves use such language, though others may. Consider, then, an illustration of how military metaphors are embedded within the discourse of educational leadership. Below is a hypothetical dialogue between a superintendent of schools, Dr. Maurice Dillon, and his principal aide, Ms. Laura Graves, as they prepare for a meeting with the board of education. The military metaphors are emphasized in this dialogue and explained after the passage. Most educators will recognize them instantly, but not necessarily know their military derivation.

PREPARING FOR A BOARD MEETING

Dillon: I'm concerned about the next meeting; the Board seems quite agitated and the board president is liable *to go off half-cocked* (f1) again on his favorite project.

Graves: I don't understand it either. I've told him it's *not a hill I would die on* (f2).

Dillon: Me neither. He doesn't seem to understand that we need to wait for the legislature to *give us our marching orders* (f3) before we *seize the moment* (f4).

Graves: If he doesn't do that, he won't be able *to take the high ground* (f5) on this issue in the community. And if he doesn't do that, it will be nothing but *a flash in the pan* (f6).

Dillon: *There's a time to fight and a time to stack arms* (f7). He just doesn't understand what it's like *down in the trenches* (f8).

Graves: I've heard that criticism of him before. If you're *not on the firing line* (f9), it's easy to support projects that aren't practical.

f1   *to go off half-cocked* refers to the position of the hammer on a rifle when half retracted, so that it cannot be fired when the trigger is pulled, and today means to be unprepared for the outcome of an effort or decision

f2   *not a hill I would die on* refers to an admonition that assault on heights puts the attackers at supreme risk and exposure, and today means that you must think very seriously about which objectives or goals you want to go after, as some are riskier than others

f3   *give us our marching orders* refers to a command decision to begin a march toward an objective, and today means to receive an official order to undertake an action

f4   *seize the moment* refers to recognition of an opportunity to deliver to the enemy an unexpected blow or attack, and today means to take advantage of an opportunity that appears, but was not anticipated

f5   *to take the high ground* refers to the admonition of most military commanders that taking the high ground gives one a superior field position, and today refers to occupying the more idealistic or moral reason for making a decision or selecting an objective or activity

f6   *a flash in the pan* refers to when the priming in a flintlock rifle went off without actually shooting the gun, and today means sudden effort that looks promising, but doesn't come to anything

f7   *a time to fight and a time to stack arms* refers to the condition when, if one is unprepared for battle, one declines to fight and waits for a better time f8   *down in the trenches* refers to a long cut in the ground for troops to take cover behind the piled dirt in front, used for defensive operations, and today refers to those involved in the day-to-day activities of the frontline workers

f9   *on the firing line* refers to a line of troops stationed to deliver a volley of fire, and today means occupying a front rank position in the major activity of an agency or organization.

This is just a brief example of how war may permeate the language used everyday in schools and among those who make policies that shape education. It is unlikely that either Maurice Dillon or Laura Graves would be aware of how they invoke war. What is most troubling is not that war metaphors are deliberately employed, but that the language of a phenomenon so abhorrent to many is used unconsciously and so may influence thinking.

THE AMBIVALENCE OF WAR METAPHORS

Common war metaphors in the literature cluster around strategy, leaders and characteristics of effective combat leaders, winning battles, the enemy, overcoming adversity, and perseverance. Metaphors about war in leadership almost always invoke heroes, or heroic actions. They are immensely seductive because they are so recognizable and nearly universal. For example, US General George S. Patton Jr. listed the qualities of a great general when he was a cadet at West Point in 1909:

1. Tactically aggressive (loves a fight)

2. Strength of character

3. Steadiness of purpose

4. Acceptance of responsibility

5. Energy

6. Good health and strength (D'Este, 1995, pp. 105–106)

So, the reader may ask, how would these qualities *not* be applicable to any leader in any walk of life? What about "loves a fight"? If this maxim were applied, perhaps as the proclivity to persist actively in the cause of better education or a fight for equity and equality in social institutions, it would certainly be appropriate and not confined to mortal combat. Centuries earlier, Sun Tzu said that leadership was a matter of "intelligence, trustworthiness, humaneness, courage, and sternness" (Sun Tzu, 1988, p. 45). Those, too, sound fairly universal.

However, when war metaphors are applied in education, they are usually used to describe the decisive or bold actions needed by administrators and agency managers, but rarely classroom teachers. The metaphors denote, implicitly or explicitly, that war casts two opposing sides. When applied to education, ambivalence enters. If "wicked issues" (Stewart, 1996), such as inequality, are the enemy, then the heroic stance accorded to military leaders may be entirely reasonable in educational leaders. Defeating injustice, underachievement, or discrimination in education lends itself to the glorifying language that is used to inspire the troops. If, however, people are on the other side, that is teachers, school principals, or those who train them in universities, then the single-minded determination of war leaders to defeat the enemy may look like something other than a morally justified, commendable attitude. Orwell (1950/1961) saw the purpose of leaders in war as quite different to that advocated by military leaders themselves:

> War is a way of shattering to pieces, or pouring into the stratosphere, or sinking in the depths of the sea, materials which might otherwise be used to make the masses too comfortable, and hence, in the long run, too intelligent. (p. 191)

Funding goes to war machinery rather than public services such as education. From Orwell's perspective, the public body thereby devises a system where opportunities are denied to the many by means that camouflage the intent. So the use of war metaphors may glorify those "fighting" the incompetent or the lazy. However, if the diagnosis of the cause of educational failure is incorrect—that is, for example, if it is not incompetent faculty members who are the cause of students' underachievement—then the heroic stance of leading the battle against them is merely a means of preventing real action to remedy the problem.

War metaphors applied to educators can therefore communicate the necessity for leaders to exhibit qualities that have been admired for millennia as reflecting the heights of individual achievement and righteousness, or, alternatively, can communicate a divisive culture where blame and defeat are the aims.

The dark side of war metaphors is largely hidden. The impact of warriors is violent, destructive. War crushes children in particular, the innocent and powerless bystanders of conflict. The use of military metaphors in education should evoke consideration of how far the two things compared, war and leading schools, are alike and unalike. However, the metaphors of war are so deeply entrenched in the discourse of education that they may in fact be dead or frozen, as defined in Chapter 1; that is, their use is so habitual that it no longer elicits any recognition that two unalike things are being compared (Cornelissen, 2002). "Strategy" is a primary example, where a term's ubiquitous use has obscured its origin in the Greek word for the art of being a general. The two things being compared through metaphor—current leadership activity and the actions of generals in war—have disappeared; instead the term is used as if its meaning were contemporary only. Yet, Goodwin (1996) suggests that "the selection of a particular metaphor will influence assumptions about the organizational entity, the focus of investigation and the way solutions are framed" (p. 13). Though military metaphors in education may be frozen or dead, and the metaphorical implications unrecognized in the language of target students, parent incursion, or battles for resources, they may sustain particular attitudes and a particular kind of relationship between people. Leaders are framed in a hostile or aggressive mode, enjoined in a process that is meant to defeat others. As Hartmann-Mahmud (2002) asserts, "metaphors go beyond mere description. They promote a specific world view" (p. 427). While school leaders may be cast in the heroic mold, those around them—students, parents, national policy makers—become enemies, targets in the field of battle.

Beckett (2003) explores the language of another professional field, that of social work, and compares what he terms "sacred" and "profane" language. "Sacred" language is the vessel of publicly espoused values, inculcated during socialization in training. Examples include words like "empowerment" and "nonjudgmental." Beckett points out that subsequent to training in sacred language, the profane emerges in the persistent use of military metaphors in the working discourse of social workers, where "operations" in the "field," directed by "front-line" staff, undertake "interventions" (p. 635). The clients so assiduously connected to the language of empowerment during training are transformed during practice into the recipients of aggressive incursions.

MILITARY ADMONITIONS, EDUCATIONAL SITUATIONS, AND CONTRADICTIONS

When educational leadership is cast in military metaphors, the difference in contexts may nullify the assumption that what makes sense on the battlefield makes sense in schools and classrooms. Table 4.1 considers how the aphorisms derived from war relate to education.

Table 4.1 illustrates how deeply problematic it is to take the characteristics assumed to be foundational to successful war and war leaders and transfer them to education. Although military metaphors are routinely applied in books on educational leadership, one winces when reminded

Table 4.1   Military Metaphors and Education

Common Military Admonitions	Possible Educational Situations	Differences and Contradictions
War should have a definite object.	Education must have more than one objective because human development is multilayered and multidimensional.	War and education are seen as means to an ends, as instruments. Some educators do not see education as a means to an end, but an end itself, whereas war is rarely seen in that light.
When you are going to fight a battle, collect your whole force. Victory is always the objective.	When you decide to do something important, put all of your efforts into it, but there is no equivalent of victory in education.	Rarely can all of the resources of a school be put into just one cause, because there is always more than one objective at work. Human development is not linear, and all of the children are never in the same place at the same time. Only our assessments of them make it appear so.
March dispersed. Fight concentrated.	While organizing to accomplish an objective or task, be sure to concentrate the necessary resources in order to accomplish that objective or task.	Educational workers such as teachers usually are idiosyncratic in their adherence to most goals and are very difficult to concentrate in one collective to accomplish any objective requiring sophisticated coordination.
Once an offense is undertaken, it must be sustained to the end, no matter how protracted or bitter.	Once the organization commits itself to a course of action (such as a reform) it should pursue to the bitter end, no matter what the consequences.	Rarely can activities be pursued that lose critical public support, because that may entail a change in the governance structure, which then prompts a change in personnel who are committed to the pursuit of an objective.
The strength of arms can be discerned by multiplying mass and rapid movement.	The success of the adoption of an innovation is simply the number of people committed to it and how fast they adopt it.	Only very superficial reforms can be adopted quickly. Reforms that entail deep-seated change take much longer to successfully adopt.

Common Military Admonitions	Possible Educational Situations	Differences and Contradictions
Never do what the enemy wishes you to do.	While there are "opponents" to actions in education, there are usually no "enemies," in the military sense.	Opposition to policies or practices often requires educational leaders to address them frontally and is therefore open to anticipated rebuttal.
It is critical that there be unity of command. There should be only one army, one center, and one chief.	The authority structure of the bureaucracy in education must be clearly delineated and preserved.	Bureaucratic authority structures do not permit rapid responses to challenges or changes and become barriers to dispersed or distributed decision making.
Always take the highest terrain of the geographical area and keep it.	Select the most difficult objectives or the most idealistic content of an issue.	In order to build momentum for change or reform, it is often advantageous to go with simpler and easier objectives in order to build an atmosphere of success and confidence in the leadership.

about the nature of combat being appropriate for a humane enterprise such as children and learning:

> War can be a gruesome business. Its incidentals are mutilation, death and destruction, its atmosphere is one of violence and pain, its consequences are suffering and bereavement, and it generates— although not necessarily among the fighting troops—casual brutality at best, vicious cruelty at worse. (Fraser, 1993, pp. 5–6)

These sentiments about war were similarly noted by General George S. Patton Jr.: "To so use the means at hand to inflict the maximum amount of wounds, death, and destruction on the enemy in the minimum time" (1975, p. 314). While some of the characteristics of the leaders of the military are similar to those in business, government, and educational administration, these "means" are not connected to General Patton's (1975) admonition to "catch the enemy by the nose with fire and kick him in the pants with fire emplaced through movement" (p. 314). Educational leaders have critics and opponents, but in civil society rarely are they enemies that must be annihilated. And military leaders, with few exceptions, are often frightfully ignorant about civilian politics and make poor leaders in situations where there are no definitive political outcomes. One thinks of

Generals Patton and McArthur, and of Churchill. A civilian leader once wrote about Douglas MacArthur, "you do not talk with MacArthur; he talks at you" (Manchester, 1978, p. 482), and after listening to him he was "a curious cocktail of earnest, decent, hopeful philosophy: a certain amount of rather long-range thinking and a good deal of highly impractical poppycock" (p. 483).

Many of the metaphors of military leadership are about gaining the upper hand through deception and surprise. These are hardly apt descriptors of leaders in a public enterprise who must gain respect and confidence and build trust and, if they resort to deception and surprise, are unlikely to gain confidence or build coalitions from the various constituencies that comprise potential followers in educational agencies. If leadership is also seen as "distributed," war metaphors are clearly inappropriate. Educational administration is a communal enterprise, one involving connecting people in positive networks designed to uplift and expand human knowledge and promote learning. It is not about suffering, pain, and destruction.

THE WAY OF THE WARRIOR IS DEATH: EDUCATION IS LIFE

CONTEXT

The influence of the military in nearly all societies is profound. Conflict continues all over the globe today, from the borders between India and Pakistan, the tribal areas of Pakistan where Al Qaeda is believed to live and work, and the Gaza Strip where the Arabs of Palestine and the Israelis have been fighting, on and off, for a hundred years. Military concepts and metaphors not only pepper the language of business, government, and education but, in some societies, the military code of conduct has actively shaped a culture and an outlook regarding life. We think here of the ancient Japanese Samurai code of the warrior called *bushido,* which to this day permeates education, the arts, and the political and social relations of Japan (see Cleary, 1991, p. 2). But the way of the warrior is the way of death. It is not so much the characteristics of the military leader that do not fit the educational enterprise, rather the ends to which those characteristics are applied. The metaphors of war and the warrior are not only contradictory to the function and purpose of renewing any society via its educational institutions, but antithetical to its continued function of caring for the young.

Military metaphors also assume that the military structure, objectives, and behaviors of the participants are congruent to the purpose of war. To use military metaphors without understanding that it is the context of the military function that provides them with their sense and meaning is to misconstrue the significance of their use in education. Critics of educational leadership who use military metaphors to describe its alleged weaknesses fail to grasp this difference. It is, to use a homely phrase, the difference between life and death. Perhaps British Field Marshall Sir Bernard Montgomery understood this better than most for, as Keegan (1982) observed, "He never shrank from confronting the ultimate truth about war: that it is won or lost with the lives of human beings" (p. 58).

The war metaphor is also deeply gendered. While there are some examples of successful female warriors in human history, from Boadicea, the Warrior Queen of the Iceni who led a revolt in Britain in 60 CE and wiped out the entire Roman Ninth Legion in battle (Walker, 1983, p. 111), to Lydia Litvak, the "White Rose of Stalingrad," who led an all-elite Russian male fighter plane squadron in World War Two and became a war ace credited with twelve "kills" (Strobridge, 1986), the way of the warrior remains predominately a macho bastion of male privilege, and so it is a gender discriminatory metaphor. That women are perceived as not fit for war is perhaps best illustrated by a saying in the French army, "In victory we are more than men; in defeat, we are less than women" (Perrett, 1993, p. 210). This old military adage makes it clear that wars are not to be won by women. In most cultures, women are more identified with nurturing and caring (Bjork, 2000), and so a perspective that elevates fighting, conflict, and domination to the highest mantle of leading leaves many of them at a supreme disadvantage, as well as being increasingly dysfunctional in an organizational world where compromise and collaboration are essential to progress. As David Tyack (2007) has observed, "Democracy is about making wise collective choices. Democracy in education and education in democracy are not quaint legacies from a distant and happier time. They have never been more essential to wise self-rule than they are today" (p. 185).

The challenge of educational leadership in the schools of the twenty-first century will require collaboration, not conquest. To refer to head teachers and principals as "commanders of an army engaged in conflicts on many fronts," as did The Broad Foundation and Thomas B. Fordham Institute's (2003) *Better Leaders for America's Schools: A Manifesto,* is to create an illusion of a simplified solution in the form of crude baton passing where all that is required to solve the ills of education is to issue clear and unequivocal commands from on high. Horvath and colleagues compared the difference between military leaders and school superintendents:

> Upper military leaders tend to have a system-level orientation rather than an interpersonal orientation. This study of superintendents suggests that superintendents have an integrated perspective, encompassing large amounts of intrapersonal and organizational tacit knowledge. This may be due to differences in job responsibilities between the two professions. (as cited in Nestor-Baker & Hoy, 2001, p. 121)

Educational institutions serving a democracy face the classic problems of dealing with dissent and ambiguity, where interests have to be met that are often contradictory to one another and where issues of schooling are, as Tyack has noted, "intrinsically political" (2007, p. 145).

Nowhere in the US is the field more political than the New York City schools, where politics have reigned supreme for decades. Powell (2009) describes the governance scene by indicating that

> Each borough president appointed a board member. The mayor appointed two, and controlled its budget. The board elected the president and hired the chancellor . . . ethnic, racial and religious rivalry insinuated themselves into many corners, and machine politics dominated some local school boards. A chancellor controlled only high schools. (p. A29)

Within this context of conflict, during one mayor's eight-year tenure, four chancellors were fired or dismissed. Clearly, within this complicated web of power and politics, to think about leading without a clear chain of command is to be presented with a nonmilitary problem. The imposition of military power or the use of military metaphors in describing how to solve problems within this context is an anachronism.

Perhaps one of the most poignant dissents on the concept of war was issued in America by General, and later first President, George Washington, a man who had witnessed war first hand:

> My first wish is to see this plague of mankind banished from the earth, and the sons and daughters of this world employed in more pleasing and innocent amusements, than in preparing implements and exercising them for the destruction of mankind. (Harnsberger, 1964, p. 353)

LEADERSHIP PRACTICE

War metaphors, warriors, and the landscape of battles over the millennia are embedded in common discourse and inevitably are refracted in the everyday language of educational leaders. Many are unaware of their derivation in the violence and bloodshed invoked by war, even as they may at an abstract level abhor the concept of war itself. While it is true that a leader in education does face conflict of all kinds, usually the only fatalities are educational ideals, ideas, and political/intellectual/conceptual opponents. To invoke the metaphors of being at war in this arena is to cross over into a realm that confuses opposition with annihilation. Those advocating war see conflict as a means to an end. Those working in democratic contexts see conflict as the grease that keeps the wheels of consensus running, a necessary ingredient to advance human progress. Leadership in education is not about silencing or eradicating the opposition, but of using differences, and even resistance, to advance more viable and inclusive practices and perspectives. This difference was clearly recognized by Ulysses S. Grant, the US Commander in the American Civil War, who wrote in his personal memoirs (1885):

> War at all times, whether a civil war between sections of a common country or between nations, ought to be avoided, if possible with honor. But, once entered into, it is too much for human nature to tolerate an enemy within their ranks to give aid and comfort to the armies of the opposing section or nation. (pp. 444–445)

War breeds intolerance for dissent, which is vital for victory, but fatal for democracy. Educational leaders are about building coalitions for consensus through negotiation, not rooting out differences to preserve purity of purpose in the ranks. This is a fundamental difference in military leadership in war and public service leadership in a democratic context in peace. It is what makes the transference of military perspectives from the battlefield to the classroom inappropriate and at cross purposes with governance in a public sector service organization in which lay citizens still play an active role. In the context where marketization has created external competition and conflict between schools (Bowe, Ball & Gewirtz, 1994), and New Public Management has created internal conflict between the leader and those led (Hood, 1995), war-like thought, language, and actions burgeon. In order for schools to remain sites of humane education, leaders need a high degree of sensitivity and of resistance to the pressures to conduct their role as if education were a battlefield.

LEADERSHIP DEVELOPMENT NEEDS

Leadership development may currently suffer from the same disjunction as social work. Sacred language is used during preparation, where the values of leaders are assumed to be founded on democratic, collegial practices that value people and especially each individual child. Postdevelopment, the profane language of war enters, as, for example, when the reality of competition for "good" students, or maintaining test scores and public reputation, appears to justify attitudes and tactics that derive from the battlefield and military leadership. Preparation and development programs might with advantage explore with students the practical implications of authentic leadership (Begley, 2003), where values are constantly negotiated and recreated on a daily basis in order to heighten awareness of the inclusion of the profane and better to protect the sacred.

5

Leadership as Sport

Sports defines a professional leader. It is precisely in answer to this question that the sports metaphor gains much of its power.

—Lessinger & Salowe (1997, p. 192)

Millions of citizens in the UK and the US annually watch sports on television, attend sports games in person, or play a sport. Among the most popular is football, which, while containing some similar characteristics in the UK and the US, is quite different in each country. Football in the UK and most of the rest of the world is, in the US, called "soccer." American football is a derivative of rugby, a professional sport in the UK but a minor sport in the US. Despite these differences, both are team sports, and it is the team sport focus that appeals to the popular imagination about the nature of leadership and the widespread use of sports metaphors in characterizing such leadership in nonsports, "off the field" settings in business and education.

Such mass public appeal accounts for why, in North America, spending on sports sponsorships approaches $11 and a half billion and goes far beyond the intention to attract a particular male market, such as by beer commercials. In fact, it is estimated that 33% of the US National Football League's regular Sunday attendees are women (Vranica & Futterman, 2009, p. B5). Television broadcasting has brought the intricacies of the American game, which is both violent and extremely technical, into the common vocabulary of everyday viewers (Cassuto, 2009), so football phrases pepper the vocabulary of business executives and work their way as well into the lexicon of educational leaders. When one hears a US executive exhort an audience with such terms as, "We have to get back to the basics of blocking and tackling," or, "When we're in the red zone we have to score more often," these derive from the football field, and such analogies would be understood by anyone remotely familiar with watching US football. Blocking and tackling is essential to move the ball toward the opponent's goal, and the red zone is all about scoring when a team is just twenty yards away from the end zone. It is difficult to score from the red zone, because the field is collapsed, and pass receivers cannot run routes of great depth, and so are easier to cover by the defense. How often a team scores from the red zone becomes a mark of their ability to "close the deal," as they say in the business world. A failure to score from the red zone connotes a significant missed opportunity. In the UK, Australia, India, and South Africa, the vocabulary of other sports is widely used in relation to leadership. For example, cricketing terms like "sticky wicket," "on the back foot," and "digging in" are commonly used to describe the position of a leader in a difficult situation.

Many leaders attest to how sports influence their ideas and the language they use. For example, former New York City Mayor and Republican candidate for US President in 2008, Rudolph Giuliani (2002), said, "Sports have played a substantial role in the development of my thinking . . . for example, the idea of teamwork, and the balance it provides, was always with me as US Attorney, during my campaigns and later as mayor" (p. 107).

SPORTS: LANGUAGE AND ACTION

We will examine why sports analogies and metaphors are so common in the vocabulary of leaders in other sectors, including education, and also the dangers of using them. We will suggest that they lead people into believing a kind of impossible dream. Sports stories are easy to understand and usually have simple explanations for being successful, such as being positive or patient with others (see Kouzes & Posner, 2002, p. 325). These bromides vastly simplify the complexities facing leaders in complex organizations such as schools, and represent what Samier (2005) has called "kitsch" management perspectives; that is, they are cheap "knock-offs" of serious books on management and leading and always promise happy endings. In the case of successful coaches, books are written after a winning season so that readers assume that what the coach is prescribing led to this happy, that is "winning," ending (see Pitino, 1997).

But first, to begin with, we have to acknowledge that a leader of a management team does have some things in common with a coach of a football team. Much of the knowledge of modern management theory rests on the theory of games, as does modern politics (see Gawthorp, 1971).

Management guru Henry Mintzberg was recently interviewed by *The Wall Street Journal* (Mintzberg, 2009) and was asked to describe the role of management in business. Mintzberg indicated that a leader managed on three planes. A leader could manage through information, people, or action. However, Mintzberg then said,

> Managing is about influencing action. Managing is about helping organizations and units to get things done, which means action. Sometimes managers manage actions directly. They fight fires. They manage projects. They negotiate contracts. (p. R2)

The parallelisms to coaching and/or managing a sports team are apparent from Mintzberg's observation. While there are many different definitions of leadership, the one that fits sports and is often applied to education is perhaps best exemplified by Josefowitz's (1980) explanation that

> leadership, authority, power, influence—all these terms are inter-connected . . . a leader has (1) the authority to decide what should happen and who should do it; (2) the responsibility to make it happen; (3) the accountability for what does actually happen. (p. 199)

This definition fits perfectly the responsibility of a coach of a team sport. The extent of the connection between coaching an athletic team and being a manager is shown in Table 5.1.

All leaders, in whatever sphere, may undertake the same kind of activities. The point of the comparison with a sports coach is that it offers a kind of physical embodiment of what is often much more abstract in other areas such as business and education. There is something very concrete about understanding how a coach selects players and places them on a field. Success is very tangible: a higher score, more goals or runs. Sports metaphors allow followers and the wider community to visualize what the school or business leader is doing with a clear, unambiguous mental picture, rather than the usual fuzzy understanding of what leaders do who are employed in, say, finance, car manufacture, or schools.

Table 5.1   Parallels Between Team Sports and Organizational
Management Situations

Situation	What Coaches Do	What Managers Do
1. Determine overall direction of the enterprise	Determine the overall approach to playing the game	Determine the overall purpose of the enterprise by asking, "What business are we in?"
2. Examine past performance of the enterprise	Examine past records and where the team did well and where it performed poorly	Examine the profit and loss ledger and other indicators of strength and weakness of the organization
3. Determine existing managerial expertise and competence	Perform a position-by-position analysis of the quality and competence of each player on the team roster. Buy, trade, or acquire new talent to shore up roster weaknesses	Review the personnel records and other indicators of individual job performance as may exist to determine position-by-position competence and expertise
4. Take actions to improve managerial expertise and competence	Determine which players can contribute and/or improve and which players need to be let go	Determine which managers can still contribute and which ones must be jettisoned through retirement or termination
5. Set new directions for the enterprise and organizational benchmarks to assess progress toward them	Develop a new team playbook and set team benchmarks	Develop a new vision and strategy for the organization and benchmarks to assess how well the organization is doing
6. Make sure people understand and are working with each other and toward the enterprise's new directions and standards	Work with players to be sure they understand what is expected of them in the new approach to the game and how their individual competence is connected to the overall team success	Develop *esprit d' corps* among key staff, provide training for those who lack the skills, and pay close attention as to how the overall team is performing

Situation	What Coaches Do	What Managers Do
7. Monitor organizational success, take actions to improve performance and members of the team who may not be doing well	Provide extra sessions of practice and teaching for those players who are lagging and who may be preventing the team from winning	Provide individual counseling and training when required; be prepared to let nonperforming members go
8. Intervene in the enterprise when things are not going well	Increase or change the nature of the practices if necessary, alter strategy or tactics on and off the field as required	Be prepared to change things, modify tactics, or try new approaches if performance is lagging
9. Be responsible for the overall performance of the enterprise	Coaches can be fired if their teams consistently perform poorly	Business CEOs can be fired if their organizations do not perform well, and, increasingly, so can educational leaders

Football is not the only team sport from which executives and leaders can draw analogies and metaphors. There is baseball, basketball, and, in the UK, cricket and rugby. From baseball we hear such phrases as "He struck out," and "That was a home run." From basketball we hear the phrase "Well, it's no slam dunk," meaning there will be nothing easy, whatever one is proposing. Many cricketing terms are so ubiquitous we may forget that they come from sport; for example, an "all rounder," indicating someone who can both bat and bowl, in general use means multi-talented, or "all out," meaning all batsmen are out, in leadership indicates feeling exhausted. Rugby offers terms, too, such as a meeting being a bit of a "scrum," which uses the image of a rugby huddle where everyone pushes to get the ball from the center to their team.

But at some point, the similarities between team sports and organizational life began to thin out and vanish. Take, for example, motivating people. Football coaches are famous for their search for gimmicks to motivate player performance. One college football coach was so angry at his team's poor performance that at halftime he drove his fist through a metal locker-room door, breaking his hand, but his team responded by going out and winning the game. Another coach drove a steamroller through his team's practice session. One professional football coach brought a tree stump and an axe to the locker room and let all his players take a whack at it, under the guise that we will "keep chopping wood." However, one player badly injured his leg when using the axe (Zaslow, 2004).

Critics of such tactics point out that motivating players for a game is not the same as motivating employees in large organizations to improve their performance over an extended time period. One of them noted that, while success is determined on the football field with yards gained and points scored, how would a secretary in a stockroom or a teacher's aide or assistant measure success? As for inspirational halftime speeches, Wake Forest University football coach Chuck Mills once said, "I give the same halftime speech over and over. It works best when my players are better than the other coach's players" (Zaslow, 2004, p. R7). The examples of coaches' tactics above have a kind of mythic or apocryphal feel. They offer a vivid picture that encourages people to believe there is a connection between the fist through a locker door and winning. As Mills's wry comment suggests, such a connection may be entirely false. Believing the story, believing that if the coach or leader can just find a good enough gimmick the team will win, establishes dangerous assumptions about how leaders, teams, and organizations work. It is falsely comforting, offering certainties in connecting action to result, which may not be at all the case even in sports, let alone in other contexts.

The thinning out of the relevance of sports metaphors is evident in other ways. Leading in sports is in many ways unlike leading in other fields. Most athletic teams are organized so that the head coach has the absolute final word on all matters. Coaching staff maintain an elaborate and well-defined hierarchy of authority, power, and control. Bobby Bowden, long-time head collegiate football coach at Florida State University, observed that a coach's position is "not a dictatorship, but it's on the verge" (Kornacki, 2009, p. B14). He also noted that, politically, "In coaching, you've got to have more discipline and you've got to be more strict and just conservative, I think. It fits with the Republicans" (Kornacki, 2009, p. B14). It is this view that fellow head collegiate coach Lou Holtz reported, of " . . . the standards that most coaches set for their players to the GOP vision of how American society ought to operate" (Kornacki, 2009, p. B14).

Then there is the masculine nature of the coaching culture. Despite the sporting audience's expanding number of female spectators and, in some cases, the growing presence of professional women's basketball or baseball teams in the US and football and cricket in teams the UK, the really national presence of team sports represents an exclusive "male only" enterprise. It is no wonder that gender stereotypes and sexual innuendos are still prevalent in team sports and carry into the language of the workplace in approved and unapproved ways (Pereira, 2009). One collegiate football coach brought a live bull into the locker room and had it castrated before his team as an example of what he wanted them to do to the opposing team (Zaslow, 2004, p. R7). Former Hewlett-Packard CEO Carly Fiorina, who became the first female to run a huge US business, dominated by male engineers and mathematicians, once stuffed a pair of socks down her trousers and reminded her audience of salespersons that "her team had just as big a set of balls as theirs did" (Harding, 2006, p. 4). Such a reference today by men or women in educational leadership positions would be highly censored. Gender discrimination has been prevalent in educational administration and remains a lingering pejorative legacy that leaders at all levels have striven mightily to erase along with discrimination on the grounds of sexual orientation and race. In exclusive bastions such as athletic teams, such references remain rather commonplace. It is part and parcel of the baggage that often goes unrecognized with the use of sports metaphors to describe leaders and leadership in nonsports workplaces.

There are other ways that using team sports analogies and metaphors distorts leading in educational organizations.

THE LITTLE "CLOSED-SYSTEM" WORLD OF AN ATHLETIC TEAM

A football, basketball, soccer, cricket, or rugby team represents an example of what organizational theorists would call a "closed-system" social structure. A closed-system model sees an organization as a specifically constructed social system designed to attain very specific goals. In the case of a sports team, the goal is well-defined and easy to understand: It is to "win." Winning is unambiguous and obvious. It can be quantified. In this type of tight social system and over time, standard operating procedures can be developed that clearly delineate the "best way" for each of the team members to respond. As Hall (1972) notes, "The tasks to be performed in the achievement of the goal are subdivided among the members of the organization so that each member has a limited sphere of activity that is matched to his own competency" (p. 15).

The clarity of this relationship between means and ends is rarely matched in other work environments in any society, except perhaps for finely tuned manufacturing assembly line workstations. In a closed system such as a football team, Hage (1965) specifies four common practices that characterize the nature of the design:

1. The complexity of the tasks or level of specialization required is known and specific training is provided to ensure that levels of efficiency are maximized.

2. The centralization of authority in a work task hierarchy where the number of persons actually involved in decision making is quite limited.

3. The level of formalization and/or standardization which leads to role codification and the permissible range of variation allowed in each.

4. The type of role stratification or status and prestige which is attached to the jobs and the rate of mobility between the low and high ranking ones. (pp. 298–320)

We see in a football team all of these four practices at work. Each player's position comes with elaborate specifications, right down to the type of height, weight, and speed required to perform well. Recruiting is based on the specifications for each position, derived from the type of offensive–defensive system chosen by the head coach to implement. For example, a multiple-option offense requires that the quarterback be able to pass and run extremely well, whereas in an offense that is essentially pass centered, the quarterback's ability to run is secondary to his ability to remain in the pass pocket and find his open receivers. In the former, mobility is required. In the latter, it is not as necessary to excel, but this type of precision is only possible in very tight and closed systems where means and ends can be related. Such a system is called "rational," and athletic teams are, if nothing else, hyperrational organizations.

The type of quantification possible in hyperrational systems is nearly impossible to attain in other occupations and work environments. For example, it is possible to quantify in American football how well a professional team has recruited players from the college draft process. Developed by a college operations management professor at Cornell University, the quality of a professional football team's draft picks can be determined by the number of plays a recruited player is on the field for during his first five seasons. A player who was on the field for 450 of his team's 1,000 offensive or defensive plays would have a snap (the number of times the ball is put into play) percentage of 45% (Albergotti, 2009). Obviously, the higher the percentage, the better, for potential recruits. The other calculation is how well the team did in the games. To recruit well, one must not only have the players on the field, but also a team that wins games.

Comparisons to Educational Systems

Educational systems have some characteristics of closed-system social structures. However, they lack the precision and clarity of the goal of an athletic team. Goals as outcomes in schools are often ambiguous and even conflict with one another, presenting formidable obstacles to closely linking means and ends together with the same consistency as a football team. Roles are not nearly so precisely chiseled out as in a football team, as the usual conditions in schools involve high levels of duplication and overlap between teachers.

Schools differ in other significant ways from sports teams. First, teachers work in relative isolation from one another, and they have at least quasi-autonomy in their workstations, a situation quite different from sports teams where everyone's movements are defined in detail on every play (see Bidwell, 1965). Teachers within schools are only loosely articulated with one another and until recently the learning of students was not a metric that was connected to their job performance record or used to determine their salary. This idea remains controversial and is not yet standard practice in school operations. Unlike football players, schools are not filmed at selected points and individual teachers evaluated as to the correctness of their assignments carried out in the overall "game." So, compared to sports teams, schools may be called only "quasi-rational" in this respect. Whether or not student testing ever assumes the clarity of "winning" remains to be seen. Some issues with that process are that all of the goals of schools are not necessarily part of any specific test. Only selected goals of schools are tested and the scores made public, and the goals of schools are often contradictory to one another, a situation that is not unusual in social service organizations. This is because the nature of the services provided emanates from legislation at many different levels over time, from budgetary strictures and priorities, and from the courts, where judicial rulings become policy. In a democracy, with competing interests buffeting schools, it is not unusual for leaders to be working at cross-purposes and for even the idea of consensus in pursuing the goals to be absent (see Hasenfeld, 1983, pp. 87–99). Imposing the rational process of planning does little to resolve such gaps and inconsistencies. The inconsistencies remain, but may be covered over in abstract language that is designed to conceal the contradictions.

THE PROBLEM OF THE CHARISMATIC COACH AS A MODEL FOR THE CEO

Successful team sports coaches are often given a sanctified place in the larger public arena and are venerated for their wisdom because their success is so well understood and is so visible. Everyone loves a winner and wants to be identified as a winner. Winning teams sell a huge amount of personal clothing with team logos and championship symbols due to this basic human need to be identified as successful. Football coaches such as Vince Lombardi of the Green Bay Packers, Don Shula of the Miami Dolphins, Pat Riley of the Los Angeles Lakers basketball team, or Sven Goran Eriksson, the England football coach, are believed to possess keen insights into everything from large-scale managerial problems to secrets on how to motivate people (players) to become champions. What the public often forgets is that coaches live in a highly controlled environment, where the linkages between performance and results are like no other place in the social world, and where such certainties bestow a distinctive aura to these very public coaches. The public comes to believe they have something very special about them. Thus begins the legacy of coaching charisma.

Charisma is more than charm. Charisma is a kind of rock-star quality. The word charisma comes from the ancient Greek and means "gift"; it refers to a gift from the gods that could not be explained in any other way. Certain "powers" were then called *charismata* (Conger, 1989, p. 22). The early Christian church used the term to apply to prophets and their extra-ordinary powers of healing.

The sociologist Max Weber (1922/1991) used the term "charisma" to describe these personal characteristics and indicated that other cultures also possessed the same idea but called them *mana, orenda,* or the Iranian word *maga,* from which the term "magic" is derived (p. 2). Whatever the term, such a special gift was bestowed on a person by others, and was not something that was innately possessed by the individual. Charismatic leaders were both good and evil. They included figures like Jesus or one such as Adolf Hitler. Charisma can be used to promote salutary causes or terrible ones. It is a gift that can be used for a variety of human ends.

The coach who comes into possession of charisma is often pursued by losing sports teams to turn around their misfortunes. Exorbitant salaries are paid to these sports franchise saviors, and similar things happen in the world of business—and, less often but increasingly, in education. When coaches or CEOs are said to possess charisma they stand above others by the bestowal of the gift. A leader who has charisma "is thus one whose right to rule is legitimated by neither tradition nor rules but rather by his apparent endowment with superior powers for solving particular problems" (Khurana, 2002, p. 156). Some CEOs come to be seen as "corporate saviors" who can pull failing organizations from the doldrums. Khurana (2002) studied the case of how failing corporations go on a fruitless search for a corporate savior, often bypassing qualified, competent, but less glamorous potential leaders and where boards of directors "discharge—or rather shun—one of their most important duties with what amounts to a belief in magic" (p. 208).

In reflection, Khurana (2002) explains that the whole process of charismatic succession in business is the idea that "there is one right person for the job" (p. 208), and he likens it to a belief in fairy tales and white knights, lone rangers, and other mythological heroes that children need in order to sleep well at night. "No single individual can save an organization" (p. 209), he cautions us, but the successful sports team coach presents the embodiment of a myth even well educated and rational people still believe in. They forget that a sports team is an aberrant microcosm that does not exist in many other places in the real world.

In education in the US, the trend is the so-called "gunslinger superintendent," who is the business equivalent of the corporate savior.

"Gunslinger superintendents" are nontraditional school leaders who are chosen to try and clean up mostly urban school systems mired in poor pupil performance, strong teacher unions, recalcitrant bureaucracies, and hostility to new ideas (Eisinger & Hula, 2008, p. 113). These new school CEOs come from business, government, the banking industry, the military, and the law, to name a few. Few ever began their careers in education, and almost none have career aspirations to move up in educational administration. They are expected to exercise "ruthless leadership that is prepared to tackle really ancient problems of management" (p. 116). As Eisinger and Hula (2008) also observe,

> The function of the gunslinger, therefore, is to ride into town and tame or even replace the school board, challenge the unions, master the bureaucracy, and for good measure galvanize students and parents to commit to higher achievement. (p. 112)

It is interesting, but not surprising, that of the 25 gunslinger educational leaders listed by Eisinger and Hula (2008, p. 114) none are women; another legacy from the world of team sports. The record of these "ruthless leaders" is quite mixed. Some have enjoyed some success, others have had their metaphorical guns removed and been run out of town (English, 2004).

Leithwood and Jantzi (2005a) place the idea of charisma in educational leaders in context. They argue that notions of transformational leadership identified charisma as an essential attribute of leadership (Bass & Avolio, 1990; Burns, 1978). More recently, theories of distributed leadership emphasize that school success comes down to more than a single individual, and that dependence on a charismatic principal is therefore a high-risk strategy.

UNDERSTANDING THE NATURE OF POWER

In his book *The Pathology of Power*, Norman Cousins (1987) speaks of the corrosive effect of power when it is not used wisely. Viewed from a historical perspective, Cousins noted that the users of power had a tendency to drive intelligence underground, distorting and damaging the traditions and institutions it was engineered to protect, and leading to a language of its own, corrupting and replacing other forms of communication. This resulted in spawning imitators and led to rival competitive forms, becoming a self-serving and exclusive theology with a proclivity to set the stage for its own purposes (pp. 23–24). We see this kind of power used by coaches in team sports, where in some professional situations players are not humans anymore, but highly paid gladiators who can be bought and sold to fight in different arenas until they are no longer capable of competition.

Cousins reminds us that, just as with a sports team, meaning and law and order exist only within that team, or in the world within the nation state. Nation states observe no laws but their own, and they act in their own self-interests. As Cousins reminds us, " . . . the self-determination of one nation is the anarchy of all" (p. 191).

While sports team metaphors will most likely continue to exert mass appeal, we should be extremely wary of using them without understanding the long legacy of the ingrained sexism and hierarchy that is part and parcel of that legacy. We do not believe it is a legacy that should be adopted in education. While there are some similarities between coaches and school leaders, as we have shown, the worlds they inhabit are actually worlds apart.

THE SPORTS METAPHOR: AN IMPOSSIBLE DREAM

CONTEXT

Our consideration of the use of sports metaphors in relation to leadership has uncovered a context where there is longing for an impossible dream; leadership where there is a kind of recidivist trust in masculine potency, where decisive action brings results, and clear wins are there for the taking through well-defined strategies and tactics. The allure of the potent leader, the (usually) male figure who knows exactly what to do and does it and wins, is a dominant figure in popular culture; Clint Eastwood's man with no name, for example. Agent 007 may have toyed with postmodernist uncertainties, but essentially in the Bond films moral certainties and the use of violence prevail. The same *zeitgeist* may underpin the popularity of sports metaphors, which reduce leadership to controllable elements and certainties. The impulse to simplify, reflected in sports metaphors, has policy implications. Korac-Kakabadse and Korac-Kakabadse (1997) suggest that the late twentieth- and twenty-first-century obsession with target setting and performance management is an attempt to manage and defeat the uncertainties and anxieties of modern life. Sports metaphors may have some part to play in creating and reflecting an environment where uncertainty and anxiety are apparently decentered and where it is thought appropriate in a field as complex and uncertain as education to produce standards that are cut and dried—education as tactics and rules.

LEADERSHIP PRACTICE

Sports metaphors can, however, offer something positive to leadership practice. In stressing that a performance is not just technical, but related to motivation and team cohesion, for example, sports may humanize leadership.

At the same time, we have argued that they are dangerous in their simplification both of practice and in their implied faith in the charismatic individual. There are multiple examples of the negative results on practice of such thinking. The football transfer approach of parachuting in a new manager who was successful elsewhere has not much record of success in English football. This has not prevented the tactic being commonly used to address schools that are underperforming, sometimes with disastrous results (Baker, 2007). One effect of metaphors is to stimulate thought about what is similar and what is different in the two things compared. Currently, educational leadership practice may be influenced too much by the similarity to sports coaching and may not give sufficient consideration to the very great differences.

LEADERSHIP DEVELOPMENT NEEDS

As argued above, it may be that development using national standards is in part driven by and reflective of a mentality related to sports. In designing development for school leaders, it might help if the clear, simple messages from sport were accepted, but also developed to incorporate a degree of complexity appropriate to education. For example if, as team coaches suggest, motivation and morale really matter, educational leadership development might study in depth the theory and practice of motivating staff. Equally, if the football/cricket/rugby manager as hero does not work, and it mostly hasn't for England's national football team, as millions of fans will testify, leadership preparation and development might with advantage begin to focus to a greater extent not on the principal, but on teamwork and distributed leadership. Sports metaphors may highlight areas of key importance, but the development of school leaders must be very different indeed from that of sports coaches. Comparing sports to schools, as might be said in the UK, is "just not cricket" in two senses; in the literal sense, they are not the same thing, and in a metaphorical sense, the comparison implies dubious values that all right-minded sports fans would deplore.

6

Leadership as Theater

Our nation's security, economy, and place on the world
stage depend on the success of our educational system.

—Markey (2004, para. 4)

The quotation by Ed Markey signals the fact that education has
become an element in political spectacle in the life of a nation, especially in the UK and the US. Political spectacle involves the use of symbolic
language, dramaturgy, the illusion of rationality, and democratic participation, separating a connection between means and ends, and a failure to
distinguish action on stage from action behind or under the stage (Smith,
Miller-Kahn, Heinecke, & Jarvis, 2004, p. 12). This chapter uses theater as
a metaphor to see with fresh eyes how education has become part of the
political landscape in the last several decades and how an emphasis on the
spectacle has worked to distort our view of the true situation in the schools
of both nations.

Theater has been used as a means to understand the world since the
ancient Egyptian religious passion plays featured the reunification of Isis
and Osiris for audiences three thousand years ago (Jacobus, 2005, p. 2).
Taken up by the ancient Greeks, similarly in religious rituals, theater began
as the actors wore masks and spoke in rhymed verse. In the evolution of
Greek drama, one of the actors broke with the ranks and spoke as an

individual, and thus began the tradition of theater. That tradition is still alive and compelling today because

> theatre . . . is not something apart from society—or something that society invented to fulfill some purpose or other. Rather, it is a crystallization and typification of what goes on in society all the time—or more sharply, what a social relationship in fact is. (Perinbanayagam, 1985, p. 63)

For example, Carly Fiorina, who went from secretary to chief executive on Wall Street, was hired as the CEO of Hewlett-Packard and within six years was subsequently fired. She describes her dismissal from H-P as a "public beheading" (Harding, 2006, p. 4). She admits to reading Sophocles's tragedy, *Antigone*, written in 441 BCE about a daughter of Oedipus who must choose between obeying human law or a higher law. From this classic Greek play she annually examined her own behavior. "Alone, and in private, I ask myself whether I am at peace with the choices I've made. Is my soul still my own?" (p. 4). Antigone is a heroine because she acts with the conviction that she is right, even as she disobeys the king who is subsequently undone by her conviction.

Carly Fiorina was using drama as the Greeks and the Jacobeans most notably used *theatrum mundi*, the world as stage, as a frequent heuristic device. It has remained "a compelling image in Western literature" (Burns, 1972, p. 8). Shakespeare's, "All the world's a stage, and all the men and women merely players," is commonplace. Every person reading this chapter is likely to be able to quote at least one famous phrase comparing the world to a stage and people to actors. The frequency with which the metaphor is used is a testament to its power to engage people imaginatively in understanding their experience. Anderson (2005) advocates that theater helps us "understand how human beings get along with each other, how they work with each other" (p. 587) and goes on to suggest that the metaphor of theater can alert us to the gulf between the performance and what lies beneath.

It is this enduring feature of theater that is the key to its power. Jacobus (2005) indicates that "drama has . . . the capacity to hold up an illusion of reality like the reflection in a mirror" but it is more than actual reality. The illusion draws upon "our potential or imagined experience" (p. 2) so that the past, present, and future are engaged simultaneously in actual and potential actions. The drama of theater is its capacity to not only reflect but to project. And it performs this magical feat almost effortlessly when done well.

This distinctive feature of theater raises interesting ontological questions related to the distinction between "the world as stage and the world as staged" (Anderson, 2005, p. 20). Might we understand a school as if it were a stage, analyzing the relationship between the phenomenon of a school and the external audience of communities that ripple out in rings from the school, and might we also understand it as staged, as a set of relationships that are performed, that is, consciously created and manipulated between the leaders, faculty, and students, among others? We use this distinction in the chapter first to explore schools as if they were a stage and, second, schools and school leadership as staged or enacted.

THE SCHOOL AS STAGE: WHAT LIES BENEATH?

The metaphor of theater directs attention first of all to schools as arenas of action and thereby alerts us to the relationship between what is happening on the stage of school and the world that surrounds it. Schools have always performed to an audience of parents, inspectors, local communities, the voting public, and politicians. However, the performative world means that the scrutiny of the audience is more intense than it has ever been. This has become even more exaggerated as many US urban school systems have seen their enrollments plunge. For example, San Antonio, Texas, has lost 25% of its enrollment in a decade, and Saint Louis 40%. These public school districts now have to pay for advertising campaigns to change the public image of urban education and try to lure students back into their classrooms (Simon, 2009b, p. A3).

The accumulation of information and data and its availability through various media, including the Web, results in potentially every member of the public watching from a first-row seat. Youell (2005) provides a historical context:

> In the early part of the twentieth century the classroom was a much more private place than it is now. In books and later in films, the classroom was characterized as a place where teacher and pupils battled it out behind a closed door, subject only to occasional, usually unwelcome, visits from the Headmaster. Parents were certainly not expected to "trespass" on school territory, unless invited to attend school ceremonies or summoned into the Headmaster's presence to account for their child's shortcomings . . . By comparison, the classroom at the beginning of the twenty-first century is a very public place. (p. 59)

As a consequence, the relationship between audience and actor has changed. To characterize the change, consider the difference between theater and film. Prior to the advent of film, theater audiences generally could view actors' gestures only as "broad brush." Subtleties of facial expression, for example, were obscure to most, if not all, in the auditorium. The advent of the huge cinematic screen allowed recognition and interpretation of even small signifiers of thought and feeling; a lift of the eyebrow, a minute change in the size of pupil in the eye. The audience consequently may feel that they know intimately the characters they watch. They feel that they can understand what each is thinking and why they act as they do. In fact, such a conclusion is false. The audience can interpret the situation and psychology of the character portrayed, but the thought or emotion each audience member attributes to the raised eyebrow is merely a momentary guess. They cannot know in a definitive way. Beneath the character portrayed is the living person who is acting. There is no relationship between the character the actor plays and the underlying psychology and actions of the person, rather than the character. Members of the audience both understand this and nevertheless persist in the belief that they "know" this character and that in some sense it reveals the actor, hence the shock when an actor who plays heroic roles is exposed in a less than heroic light in the press.

This is easily applicable to schools. An early example is teachers' subjection to the Madeline Hunter model. Smyth (1989) interviewed 200 teachers involved in this initiative in Pennsylvania and discovered that the surveillance scheme "promoted a form of 'ritualism' which teachers failed to take seriously; it concealed their personal and professional histories through episodic visits by outside experts" (p. 343). The visitor and those using the results of the scrutiny of teachers appeared to "know" the faculty members. What they in fact knew was the ritualized performance offered to the visiting experts. Just as an audience knows that what it views is a fabrication but nevertheless persists in believing in its truth, so inspections, whether of the Madeline Hunter model or any other, are acknowledged to be public rituals and acted upon as if they result in a valid understanding of faculty and schools.

Such a relationship between schools and the public has continued and intensified. The perceived lesser distance between school and parents, and local and national policy makers, has resulted in a conviction that the school is known in intimate detail. The published league tables, examination results, prospectuses, and inspection reports can all support the illusion of knowing the school. The practice that is "known" is carefully performed. There are frequent references in the literature on school surveillance to Bentham's (1787) panopticon, the aim of which was to make prisoners feel that they were constantly overseen, whether they were or not. In response, prisoners ensured that their behavior was acceptable at all times, because they could not know the exact moment when they were being watched. Warders knew that the prisoners' behavior was a projected performance that may have concealed far less acceptable thoughts and activity. In schools, the careful presentation of practice is captured by the metaphor of a play, specifically crafted for external view (Perryman, 2006; Ball, 1997), with the audience colluding by suspending disbelief and responding as if the fabrication were the reality.

This collision of life and art into a form of public theater has evolved over the past several decades as noted by Gabler (1998)

> After decades of public-relations contrivances and media hype, and after decades more of steady pounding by an array of social forces that have alerted each of us personally to the power of

performance, life has *become* art, so that the two are now indistinguishable from each other . . . the deliberate application of the techniques of theatre to politics, religion, education, literature, commerce, warfare, crime, everything, has converted them into branches of show business, where the overriding objective is getting and satisfying an audience. (pp. 4–5)

The line between theater and real life is becoming increasingly indistinct. In schools, we sometimes see much school leadership activity, such as in the UK preparation for inspection or the presentation of data, as a performance designed to control what is revealed and what is concealed. As Perryman (2006) asserts, "the whole school effort is directed away from education and toward passing inspection" (p. 146). She provides an account of a school (Northgate) in England that was placed in special measures, that is, deemed to be below an acceptable standard and subject to an Office for Standards in Education (Ofsted) inspection. She charts the ways in which teachers' behaviors and school documents were changed to meet what it was believed the inspectors would approve, saying,

> At Northgate teachers believed they must act as if they were being inspected all the time, in order to "train" themselves and pupils into expected modes of behaviour, and so that the arrival of an inspector would be seen as normal. (p. 155)

Concise and practice-focused documents were enlarged to reflect fulsomely the values and practice that national guidance documents prescribed. Lessons were compliant to a strict model: "a 'good' lesson increasingly resembled a driving test, in which failure could result from one incorrect three-point turn despite the success of all the other manoeuvres" (p. 157). One senior manager noted that they were told to set up a system to prove that everyone was improving, so they did and it impressed the inspectors. Evidence that such behavior is widespread in England is provided by Earley (1998), whose study of inspection concludes that "the nature of the audit influences performance, and schools change their practices to conform to what they think the inspectors inspect" (p. 172). Words like "perform" or "show" are used repeatedly in studies of inspection. Boorstin (1987) has called these types of theatrical situations "pseudo-events," and defines them as

> a happening that is not spontaneous, but comes about because someone has planned, planted, or incited it . . . it is planned primarily . . . for the immediate purpose of being reported or reproduced [and] arranged for the media. . . . Its relation to the underlying reality of the situation is ambiguous. (pp. 11–12)

The theatrical metaphor directs our intention more emphatically to the gulf between the performance of characters and actions and the different beliefs and intentions of the actors. Was everybody indeed improving? The words of the senior manager suggest that this was not the case, but that the "system" they performed gave this illusion very successfully.

The power relations between actors and audience have always been fluid. The audience pays and can be fickle in what it approves. However, the actors can hold the audience spellbound, removing them from their everyday reality, moving to a world that both inhabit but that the actor creates and controls. Galbraith (1983) analyzed three forms of power: condign, which is based on manipulation through threats; compensatory, which manipulates through rewards; and

> Conditioned power, in contrast [to condign and compensatory power], is exercised by changing belief. Persuasion, education, or the social commitment to what seems natural, proper, or right causes the individual to submit to the will of another or of others. The submission reflects the preferred course; the fact of submission is not recognized. Conditioned power, more than condign or compensatory power, is central . . . to the functioning of the modern economy and polity, and in capitalist and socialist countries alike. (pp. 5–6)

The surveillance regimes discussed above are a means of exercising conditioned power. Leaders and faculty accept that playing games with inspectors and performing their school, with all the limitations and manipulation of behavior that this implies, is an inevitable part of leading schools in the twenty-first century. As Galbraith argues, unconscious submission to normalized discourse and practice may be the primary source of power in current times. However, threat and reward also have their place. The theater metaphor can be used to sharpen our analysis of the use of such power. The public exposure of failure in league tables and inspection reports tarnishes the school's performance and renders it subject to the disapproving gaze of parents and community. The play is booed. By contrast, "excellence," at least in performing for inspection as required, can lead to applause: self-vaunting articles in the local press, quotations from the inspection report in the prospectus and on the website, and letters home to parents boasting of success. The performance of success is polished and projected with gusto.

What lies beneath may be different: the actors and their lives, rather than the play. Using the theater metaphor differently, Beecher (1989), drawing on Bailey (1977), distinguishes front stage, backstage, and understage to indicate arenas for action in education. Front stage is the public arena, the backstage is where deals are done, and under the stage is where gossip is purveyed (p. 321). The metaphor of three stage areas is powerful in crystallizing the nature of leadership as resulting from a flow of formal and informal, publicly discernible and obscure interactions. Beneath the razzle-dazzle of the play about success may lay the backstage machinations to project a consistent plot, such as the system that proves everyone is improving

(Perryman, 2006). Under the stage may lie the deeply damaging effects on individual students and faculty, as they experience the effects of pressure from a performative environment (Jeffrey, 2002; Youell, 2005).

THE SCHOOL AS STAGED: LONG RUN OR REPERTORY?

The metaphor of school as a stage is powerful in releasing multiple points of similarity between the two things compared. Consider the nature of the long-running play and a series of plays in repertory. Famously, Agatha Christie's thriller, *The Mousetrap,* has run on the London stage for over fifty years. The audience is aware of its history and may view the play in a context of culture and values that stretches back half a century. Sets and costumes may be refreshed, but the core characters and script remain the same and appeal sufficiently to the audience for them to keep buying tickets. By contrast, repertory relies on a constant flow of what is novel, so that an audience engages for a brief period with characters and ideas and then casts them aside for the latest offering. This method is, of course, particularly true of film, where the latest blockbuster is assumed to be needed to refresh jaded palates and win audience applause. The point of both the long run and repertory is at least in part to make money; to capitalize.

The performance of schools is both long run and repertory. Nation states produce an endless succession of revised or new policy, so that the surface performance of schools appears constantly mutable. The curriculum, assessment, and additional services for children demand the constant busyness of faculty to implement what is mandated and equal busyness from commentators and analysts attempting to keep up with the latest. Whatever the parade of change across the stage, the world outside the theater is not affected by the play. It has its own rhythms and constancies, of socioeconomic class, of gender expectations, or of poverty and wealth. Education may serve as the kind of escape valued by theater audiences, where momentarily ongoing life and its challenges are left behind. Policy makers, faculty, and communities join to construct schools as places where, normatively, children are helped to fulfill their potential. Quantz and Rogers (1991) point out that there is overwhelming research evidence that "schools work for the very special interests of the status quo" (pp. 3–4). In both the UK and the US, evidence suggests that, for all the performance around equality, social justice, and raising standards, the deterministic effect of socioeconomic class and race remains as strong as ever. Bourdieu (1984) has even suggested that one of the implicit missions of the schools is to naturalize cultural and class differences and convert them to "natural" differences so that such distinctions are seen not as social constructions consisting of arbitrary power and domination, but as "the way things are" (p. 68). Demack, Drew, and Grimsley (2000) show that in a period of intense political activity to raise standards, "between 1988 and 1995, attainment differences relating to social class, ethnicity and gender are all seen to increase" (p. 117). To misquote Hamlet, "the play is not the thing." The activities of schools, the performance of policy change, equality, and transformation are a repertory run that may distract by offering an alternative reality to that outside the school, where inequality continues and lack of change persists. The long run, with consistent culture, values, action, and inequality, persists.

THE SCHOOL AS STAGED: ACTING LEADERSHIP

The use of metaphors of theater and acting is ubiquitous in relation to explorations of identity and to creating an identity as leader. One of the most influential writers on identity, Goffman (1959), reflected on his writing:

> I spoke of performers and audiences; of routines and parts; a performance coming off or falling flat; of cues, stage settings and backstage; of dramaturgical needs, dramaturgical skills, and dramaturgical strategies. (p. 246)

Over forty years later, Collinson (2003) sees the context as having changed, in that the result of "the gaze. . . . [of] routinized surveillance is 'heightened self-consciousness.'" He sees the result as workers using a "dramaturgical self" (p. 186), the use of this term illustrating the continuing power of the theater metaphor in helping to unravel the complexities of identity.

There is a substantial literature considering how and why individuals create and manage identities, that is, multiple alternate self-concepts, which are designed to seek the approbation of self and others and deflect disapproval or resistance. While theory drawn from a range of disciplines including, among others, social anthropology (Mead, 1934), sociology (Bauman, 2004), and psychology (Gudykunst, 1995), can be used to provide insights, metaphor, and particularly that of the theater, provides a pathway to engage imaginatively and emotionally with the implications of leadership identity.

Every person is many persons within themselves:

> Within each of us there are a number of different persons simultaneously. We are one person in the secret part of our minds, in fantasy or thought, we are another person when we are alone within the comfort zone of our homes, and we are still another person when we are with friends and loved ones. We assume many other "selves" within a variety of environmental situations. (Lessinger & Gillis, 1976, p. 55)

This quotation indicates that, as individuals, we are used to role playing, though we may not be aware of it. Starratt (1993) noted, "We are constantly playing out the drama from scripts of our own creation, or scripts we have learned from our own environment. We assign roles to ourselves and to the antagonists in our lives" (p. 113). As we learn to slip in and out of multiple roles in different situations, we do not consider ourselves phony for doing so. Leadership is a role. Even though a person may not officially be a leader in an organizational hierarchy, the individual may still take on this part. Leaders learn to project different faces within the role in which they are cast.

Though leadership can be undertaken by many, at least according to distributed leadership theory (Spillane, Halverson, & Diamond, 2004), the educational leadership role is most notably and publicly undertaken by the principal/head teacher or superintendent. Having taken the part, the leader may consciously or unconsciously work to create one or more leadership self-concepts and project them in numerous arenas. Consider, for example, the creation of the *curriculum vitae* or resume. It is increasingly a work of art, where the positive communication of achievement may strain at the limits of truth. Collinson (2003) also argues that the virtual environment provides a ready tool to manage who is told what and to create identity:

> By reconfiguring time and space, technologies like email and cell phones can facilitate dramaturgical claims by leaders and followers about where they are, what they are doing, and even who they are. In addition, on-line and email protocol raises further questions about the strategic and political nature of communication. This is not just in relation to the content of messages, but also regarding who is being emailed, who is copied in, and who is excluded. (p. 186)

Equally, the office is a set for performance, and the costume of dress contributes to the careful construction of a leadership self (Goffman, 1959).

The leadership role has audience expectations. The strength of these is most clearly perceived if, as Goffman (1959) claims, the leader is caught in *flagrante delicto*, stepping outside the role expected by a specific audience. For example, a student entering the social area for faculty might be startled to see behavior quite outside that offered as a public identity in class. Equally, faculty would be perturbed to be caught outside the role. It is as if a member of the audience has crept into the wings during the play and caught the actor swigging a drink, or scratching, or any other behavior "incompatible with the impression that they are, for wider social reasons, under obligation to maintain to the intruder" (p. 204).

Consider the behavior of a leader at a parents evening. Normatively, the principal may project a mix of authority, care for all students, and respect for parents. A range of research suggests a different relationship between parents and faculty. Phillips (2005) analyzes the empirical research and suggests that "the harmonious, anodyne relationships presented in many of the parental involvement texts . . . are characterized by a struggle for control and definition" (p. 27). From different parts of the world, the domination of the professional emerges. There is evidence from New Zealand that "partnership" with parents is generally on the terms of the professional (Robinson & Timperley, 1996), and evidence from Scotland that engagement is about "parents helping teachers to achieve goals specified by teachers in ways specified by teachers" (McCreath & Maclachlan, 1995, p. 71). The performance of leaders and faculty at meetings with parents keeps parents distanced and with lesser power. Just as an actor's power over an audience would be dented if the audience glimpsed the actor beneath the character, so the school leader maintains a role implying both greater knowledge than others (professionalism) and equal care for all (objectivity rather than partisanship). Goffman (1959) expounds the intended effect of the performance:

> A correctly staged and performed scene leads the audience to impute a self to a performed character, but this imputation—this self—is a *product* of a scene that comes off, and is not a *cause* of it (pp. 244–245, original emphasis).

Students, parents, and the wider community are encouraged to read qualities into the leadership performance that may or may not be congruent with other identities, as ambitious professional, as family person, as member of the middle class, as a white man, and so on. While there is evidence of leaders behaving in ways that appear to support a performed identity, for example, privileging students who are disadvantaged, there is also evidence of the opposite. In a study of four regions in England and Wales (Lumby & Morrison, 2009), many high school students believed that schooling was so shaped to further advantage those already advantaged by socioeconomic class or by academic attainment. Those who struggled academically were sidelined, evidenced by the experience of numerous students in Lumby and Morrison's (2009) study. One student believed, "In school the teacher explains and then says if you don't understand put your hand up, but if you put your hand up, they have a go at you" (pp. 7–8). Another explained, "I ask for help and the teacher just blanks me out and helps someone else" (pp. 7–8). One young man summarized the position: "They help the ones who know" (p. 8). Those who arguably least need help get the most.

Leaders are aware of such inequalities and may resist or be complicit in sustaining them; for example, the intention to improve the school by attracting more "good" students, or discouraging or blocking the entry of those who may be challenging in terms of the extent of support required for their behavioral or learning needs. In this way, the audience of students and parents for the leadership performance may be shaped as far as is feasible. The performance of school leadership as a benign caretaker offering equitable support for all students is challenged by considerable evidence, for example of racism and sexism (Gillborn, 2004, 2005; Osler, 2004; Quantz & Rogers, 1991; Rusch, 2004). Nevertheless, so powerful is the performance of school leadership that the audience is drawn into believing the projected identity. The leader becomes the performed identity (Goffman, 1959). Bertolt Brecht (Brecht & Willett, 1964) developed a theory of theater, *Verfremdungseffekt*, with a contested English translation, but often understood as distancing the audience. Brecht suggested that, rather than identify with or become lost in the performance of the actors, an audience should be induced to remain detached, so that emotion and closeness do not cloud judgment about the social and political forces that shape the lives of protagonists. It may be that social justice would be better served if both the performers of school leadership and the audience of the performance were encouraged to be more critical of the performance and its congruence with the evidence of behavior to staff and students. School leaders are, of course, in receipt of a good deal of critique for not matching the standards as specified in national policies, but rarely for the congruity or dissonance of their values as performed in their leadership identity.

The performance is embodied in language, and leaders learn the script (Lumby & English, 2009). Starratt (1993) indicates that culture provides a kind of rough draft for performance inasmuch as it provides clues about how to behave in certain kinds of situations, but without specific lines in a script. Leaders invent the specific words, but the lines generally "fit in" with expected cultural casting (p. 121).

Sturdy, Brocklehurst, Winstanley, and Littlejohns (2006) studied the preparation of generic leaders and concluded that the primary aim of their Master of Business Administration (MBA) program was to achieve literally a confidence trick; that is, for leaders to emerge able to project confidence in themselves as leaders, rather than primarily acquiring any particular skills of leadership:

> . . . conventional notions of acquiring, translating and applying management tools and frameworks are barely significant. Rather, what we might consider to be the learning of explicit management knowledge is more the development of a form of self-confidence, but a form which both disguises and reproduces the fragility of knowledge and identity. In this sense, it might be seen as a "trick" of confidence in that it is not so much what you know, but what you and others think and feel that you know and can say. (p. 844)

The result of the leadership program was, as one student expressed it, "I perform quite differently now." (Sturdy, et al., 2006, p. 850), or another: "I don't think the learning is very deep. I think you can be more convincing by the way that you talk" (p. 851). The leadership program was a form of training to perform the script. This study is of an MBA for leaders of business and industry, but the emphasis on learning to perform is clearly visible in preparation for school leadership. The chief executive of the National College for School Leadership in England gave a speech at the annual conference in 2009 (Munby, 2009). He suggested that head teachers "put on the mantle of leadership . . . [and] step into the role" (p. 1) with "many different but critical roles to play" (p. 1) and that "one of our chief roles as leaders is as storyteller" (p. 19). The confidence trick is visible also: "Being an effective leader means we first have to believe in our own leadership" (p. 1), even though "we may secretly worry that some day someone will find us out, but we wear that cloak of leadership" (p. 2). The fabrication in the performance is also evident:

> Isn't it funny that many heads tell me that their leadership team is the best in the region or even the country? Provided that you think you have a great leadership team, that's good leadership. (p. 19)

Having encountered very many heads who claimed their team was the best, the projection of logically a false picture, in most cases, since not all can be the best, was applauded as doing the leadership job effectively. This high-profile speech about school leadership makes clear the imperative of leadership to provide a performance of cheerfulness, of working for the good of all, of persuading others to a vision that is palpably overoptimistic. It is the equivalent to the musical, where everyone feels better for viewing it by the end, comforted that all turned out well. The danger is that we start to believe in it as relating to reality outside the auditorium, and not as a created performance to elicit positive emotion rather than rational thought.

THE SCHOOL AS RITUAL PERFORMANCE

The relationship between the play and the audience has been of central interest throughout history. For the Greeks, plays were performed for the gods with the earthly spectator merely taking advantage of the spectacle. Drama was a way of sustaining a relationship with the immortals through enacting the fundamental and mythic dilemmas of being human. Issues of fidelity, revenge, trust, and fateful circumstance reverberate through Aeschylus, Euripides, and Sophocles. Arguably, drama migrated to the quasitheater of sacred events in the Middle Ages. In Christian societies, the liturgy enacted a spectacle with a similar aim to that of Greek tragedy; to cement a relationship with God and to stimulate reflection on what it means to be a frail and erring human. Schools of today may seem to be a long way from such dramatic and quasidramatic performances. However, much school activity has a ritual element that connects it to external forces, though in this case to a different kind of godlike power.

Ritual is characterized by Burns (1972) as "a system of communication" (p. 208) and ceremonial as customary rituals performed at moments, often quasireligious, of change. For many children, schooling is a performance of ritual where habitual enactment communicates relationships and values. Consider, for example, the young adults in the study of high school students in the UK in 2008, for whom lessons were a mysterious enactment of copying notes that were then discarded (Gorard et al., 2009), or the high school students in Harris, Wallace, and Ruddock's (1995) study, for whom school was a question of keeping up with listening, taking or making notes, and regurgitation that had little to do with understanding or learning. Such a process is designed not for the young person, but for an external audience. The quasireligious element of performance has disappeared, but the demands of utilitarianism, the economy, and international league table competition as exerted by the capitalist state may be as demanding and incomprehensible to the student actors as were the actions of the gods in ancient Greek civilization.

SCHOOL AS THEATER

CONTEXT

The school as play emphasizes the existence of an audience. There is, of course, much writing about the panoptic power of surveillance in our current society and in education (Alexander, Anderson & Gallegos, 2005; Boje, 1996; Koskela, 2000; Perryman, 2006; Selwyn, 2000), tracing roots back to Bentham (1787) and Foucault (1977). However, because surveillance through testing, data collection, and electronic means is so pervasive, we may increasingly disregard its power, forgetting its operation as we continue with our lives. We may experience it as Koskela (2000) describes: "The gaze without eyes" (p. 245). Theater provides a vocabulary (Cornelissen, 2004) to render the ubiquitous but invisible a focus for concern. It has directed us to regard the context of education as multilayered and to probe beneath the polished performance surface of cheerful, benign on-stage activity to consider the effects of the context on individual students, on faculty, and on instruction. We learn that the effect is corrosive. Bussert-Webb (n.d.) writes of her experience in high-stakes testing, of the fear of faculty and administrators that they would lose their job. The restrictive effect on instruction was also clear in her school and elsewhere. For example, Opfer (2001) places the responsibility for the continuing decline in outcomes for charter schools in Georgia with the etiolation of innovation caused by accountability measures. Under stage, the effect on our children from kindergarten infants (Youell, 2005) to older school students (Jeffrey, 2002) is crushing. The metaphor of theater brings into sharp relief the reality of the audience and the multiple arenas on which action and its impact evolves. It adds to research-based calls for a loosening of the accountability regime (Johnson, Johnson, Farenga, & Ness, 2008), a renewed sense of the urgency for change, and of the individual and social cost if the performance pressures continue.

LEADERSHIP PRACTICE

The theater metaphor directs us to distance ourselves from leadership practice—to view it as a role that projects what the audience requires. Through the vocabulary of theater we learn that, for all the writing about authentic leadership (Begley, 2003), the state apparatus exacts the opposite; that leaders create a surface product for public gaze by shaping what faculty and children do in ways that satisfy expectations. Further, in adopting the "mantle of leadership" (Munby, 2009, p. 1), leaders are enjoined to collude in suspending awareness of what is going on under stage, and to present their identity, rather as Hollywood stars, restricting any view of that which challenges the public persona. In this, leaders may be consciously cynical, for example in stage-managing inspection, or unconsciously adapting to the formidable pressures of the public view and with eyes turned away from what sustains the performance.

LEADERSHIP DEVELOPMENT NEEDS

Increasingly, the development of leaders is designed to aid them to match the activity and outcomes as specified in national standards (Lumby & English, 2009). Programs that challenge them to consider their identities, the political context within which they work, or the sociological nature of schooling and how it is structurally present in schools, are not common, and those that question the linkages may be politically ostracized (Smith, Miller-Kahn, Heinecke, & Jarvis, 2004). Generally, leader preparation and development focuses firmly and deliberately on what happens on stage and expects this to be taken as the only reality. Leaders enter into leadership, becoming the character, taking on the role. Perhaps programs need to strive for the *Verfremdungseffekt* of Bertolt Brecht. Rather than inducing confidence in knowledge of schooling and in leadership personas, programs may need to destabilize leaders, to ask them to look at their practice as leaders as strange, alien, and with potentially negative, as well as positive, effects.

In Stanislavski's book, *An Actor Prepares* (1936/1989), he describes the preparatory work of an actor in developing the inner life of the character he or she is to portray. The actor becomes the character, the better to draw the audience into viewing the performance as a reality in itself, not watching a performance but seemingly watching life. There appears to be a parallel with how school leaders are prepared when they become the leader, and students, parents, and faculty relate to this persona as a reality complete in itself. Programs might with advantage adopt more recent post-structuralist perspectives and encourage all those concerned with leadership in education to deconstruct the implications of leadership techniques, and to work toward a critical and distanced view, rather than submerging in the play of leadership.

Starratt (1993) speaks of the advantages of considering educational leadership as a form of theater when he notes, "Seen from the dramaturgical perspective leaders should have a sense of what the drama is. That is to say, they will be able to name it and thereby give it greater intelligibility" (p. 131). And, like theater, leadership in schools is a human construct to be made to serve good or evil, socially just or unjust ends, or democratic or totalitarian means to those ends for, as Ingmar Bergman (1990) observed,

> The theatre is carried by the strength of its actors. Directors and art directors can do whatever they want; they can sabotage themselves, the actors, and even the playwrights. When the actors are strong, that's when the theatre thrives. (p. 321)

The same can be said for the leadership in schools.

7

Leadership as Religion

> . . . religion has been an attempt to find meaning and value in life.
>
> —Armstrong (1993, p. xix)

A consideration of leadership and religion seems entirely *apropos* in understanding how leaders make meaning of their work and how they find the lessons of faith important in defining, guiding, and sustaining it. Banks (2000) makes the connection between leadership and faith by reminding us that "the classic theological understanding of faith is that it is more a gift from God than a human capacity" (p. 4). He goes on to say, "All human faithfulness ultimately depends on the conscious acknowledgment or unconscious influence of God's faithfulness, and it tends to manifest itself most in a person's life where there has been an ongoing experience of it in a variety of settings and circumstances" (p. 9).

Gauging the impact of religion on the metaphors of leadership involves not only those who actively and with conscious effort link their religious beliefs with their work, including inserting those beliefs into the political and social life of secular society, including schools (Kaplan, 2004; Lugg, 2000), but those of a less conscious religious bent who invoke metaphysical or faith-based metaphors in their work as school leaders.

None other than Bertrand Russell (1986), a self-proclaimed agnostic, wrote, "Acts inspired by religion have some quality of infinity in them. . . . The beliefs which underlie such acts are often so deep and so instinctive as to remain unknown to those whose lives are built upon them. . . . It is the quality of infinity that makes religion, the selfless, untrammeled life in the whole which frees men from the prison house of eager wishes and little thoughts" (p. 95).

The roots of religion in the course of humanity on earth run very wide and deep. They extend back into the mists of prehistory. What remains of beliefs of those prerecorded times are solemn artifacts such as cave paintings in France, lonely figures on remote Pacific islands, and mysterious stone symbols on the sand hills of Peru. The influence of religion in human affairs remains profound, even in countries that are hostile to some forms of it. For example, Micklethwait and Wooldridge (2009) note that in China today there are approximately a hundred million Christians, and more people go to church on Sunday than belong to the Communist Party.

Max Weber (1991/1922) in his classic work, *The Sociology of Religion,* observed that the roots of religious belief and action were centered on certain magical properties that some persons appeared to possess. Weber's observance was not to imply that the possession of that magic was somehow nonrational. In fact, he insisted that "religiously or magically motivated behavior is relatively rational behavior" (p. 1), because it adhered to the laws of human experience. As discussed in Chapter 5, Weber called the attribute of a person blessed with such magic "charisma" and proffered there were two kinds. One was simply a gift that a human being acquired at birth. The other referred to magic that was produced by an object or by an extraordinary experience. Very early in the earthly human trajectory, the presence of charisma was thought to lie behind these specially endowed persons or be contained in unique objects. Charisma was powered by "spirits," and these were not observable, but felt. We see in the traditions of Islam, for example, a long history of such observations before Muhammad the Prophet encountered the Angel Gabriel and was commanded to write the Qur'an (Koran) (Armstrong, 1992, p. 83).

The point here is that expressions of magic that, according to Weber, anchor the establishment of nearly all revealed religions, are a long-standing tradition in human life, and we find Weber's distinction of the difference between a prophet and a priest important in understanding metaphorical lineage to religion in educational leadership. Weber (1991) indicates that a prophet is a person who claims a mission and a doctrine based on his "power simply by virtue of his personal gifts" (p. 47). Weber indicates that the presence of a doctrine or belief system is what marks a prophet, and not the presence of magic. Prophets do not receive their work from distinctly human agencies or institutions. Rather, prophets "seize" their mission in an act of power directly from God, however God speaks to them. The mission of the prophet is to convince humans to conform to the vision he has received or created from the Divine, and to use whatever form is available in that process. In the words of Weber (1991):

It [the form] always contains the important religious concept of the world as a cosmos which is challenged to produce somewhat a "meaningful" ordered totality, the particular manifestations of which are to be measured and evaluated according to this requirement. (p. 59)

We shall see how standards for educational leaders assume the very same posture and outlook. Priests, on the other hand, derive their power by working within an extant prophecy and mission. They are devoted followers of a prophet and they toil within the traditions, expectations, and rules to maintain a cohesive community. While they do not create such a thing as canonical scripture (like the Bible or the Koran), they establish an interpretation. This becomes the basis of religious dogma. So, in essence, prophets seize a position based on their insights and revelations, usually at odds with existing dogma of the day, and priests work within the prophecies, mediating between the scriptures and other holy writings and create the rules by which the prophecy is applied.

THE CONCEPT OF THE EXTERNAL SUPREME BEING

At least in the Western religions, notably Judaism, Christianity, and to some extent Islam, the Supreme Being or *Yahweh/Elohim* (Jehovah) began as a local deity and was subsequently promoted or advanced as the fortunes of the group who paid tribute to him progressed and its power increased. In Islam the local god was al-Llah. In Israel, *Yahweh* was the god of war. Those who pushed his supremacy had a difficult time, because there were other gods worshipped by Israelites such as Asherah, Ishtar, Anat, and Baal who enjoyed large followings of women, since *Yahweh* was distinctly male. Later, when *Yahweh* became the only God, women were relegated to second-class citizens (see Armstrong, 1993, p. 50).

There were profound differences between the Jewish and Christian concept of God and that advanced by Muhammad regarding al-Llah. Armstrong (1993) indicates that al-Llah was more impersonal than *Yahweh*. The world was a place to see with a sense of wonder and to see beyond the obvious fragments to that which was behind it, a transcendent reality that was embedded in all things. In Islam, "God was experienced as a moral imperative" notes Armstrong (1993, p. 143). To some, such as Hegel, *Yahweh* was a tyrant who required unquestioned obedience to a set of laws. Both Jews and Christians seem to cast Him as a divine despot who must be appeased at all times (Armstrong (1993, p. 352). In this sense, God was completely external to the life of humans and only required of them total belief, devotion, and servitude. It is this posture of God to humans that has permeated much of the Western mindset and worked its way into secular thinking as the adoption of perfection as a leadership mantra.

TOWARD PERFECTION: THE IDEA OF PROGRESS

One almost universally accepted idea in the secular world represents the epitome of religion, and that is the concept of progress and a related notion of perfection. Both of these ideas are represented in the way educational leadership is conceptualized today. First, the idea of progress is that humankind has moved from a primitive condition to a more advanced state and, indeed, is on some sort of continuum toward perfection. It is not simply increasing one's knowledge. Rather, it is represented in the idea of a moral state, that is, human beings increase their goodness and thereby work toward perfection of human nature. Perhaps one of the more modern versions of this idea was advanced by Albert Schweitzer (1965), who wrote, "The linking of Christianity and purposeful affirmation of the world produced the culture in which we live. To preserve and to perfect it is our task" (p. 16). This amounts to an act of faith, in that it is possible to attain moral perfection and, as Nisbet (1970) observes, "Quite obviously, so sweeping a proposition as the idea of progress . . . cannot be empirically or logically verified" (p. 6).

MANIFESTATIONS OF RELIGION IN MANAGEMENT AND EDUCATIONAL LEADERSHIP

Stephen Pattison (1997) of the UK, who has been a senior lecturer in the School of Health and Social Welfare at the Open University, has been a management specialist and a theologian. He examines the nature of contemporary managerial thinking from a religious perspective. First, he observes that the two-thousand-year tradition of Christianity has thoroughly permeated key questions that confront humans in every corner of the globe. He avers that one does not have to be a Christian or even practice Christianity to be influenced by the thought patterns of Christian faith. Christian writing and dogma have dealt with such issues as determining the kind of world we inhabit; the nature of beliefs we espouse and how they pertain to the good life and living; the nature of the responsibilities we use toward believers and nonbelievers, insiders and outsiders; and how we discern issues of good and evil in the world (p. 56).

Pattison (1997) points out that the only real tool management has is that of language (p. 44). The role of management is to sketch out the gaps between a desired world and the one in which we live. Management's use of signs and symbols and their myriad manifestations in visions, missions, slogans, goals and objectives, evaluative systems, mediating disputes, planning, evaluating, and defining resources and costs and providing the motivation to develop and employ them are linguistically centered. He notes that, while management usually shrouds its beliefs in "tough, practical-sounding talk and scientific-seeming techniques and technologies, it is full of metaphysical beliefs and assumptions . . . often unsupported by any kind of evidence" (p. 26).

The function of management and why it can be compared to religion is that the latter offers a system of symbols that establishes enduring moods and perspectives of humans by offering a set of definitions and convictions that create the rules for existence. The rules are then set within a sphere of facticity, so that they appear to be timely and realistic (Geertz, 1993, p. 90). Management has very similar functions and, Pattison (1997) speculates, "the managerial 'revolution' . . . has been as much a rhetorical event as anything else" (p. 59).

THE PRESENCE OF "MANAGEMENTSPEAK" AND RELIGIOUS RITUALS IN SCHOOL PRACTICES

Pattison (1997) has analyzed the language of what he terms the "new management." He finds in language, and especially in the popular TQM (total quality management) ideology, words and terms that are low in definition; vague and imprecise in their exact content, easy to say; colorful and radical-sounding in metaphorical terms; and are action words that are polysyllabic so that "they sound complicated, technical and difficult to understand" (p. 61). Samier (2005) has called it "managementspeak" when it is used in paperback books, and "kitsch management," as defined in Chapter 5, meaning a trashy knock-off, pseudo-art, and something in bad taste. Airport book nooks are filled with examples of them. Samier (2005) indicates that "kitsch" management books require no knowledge or independent analysis. They are predigested and prepackaged and do not question the status quo in terms of sociopolitical relationships; they reinforce existing prejudices, avoid unpleasant encounters, and promise a happy ending (Samier, 2005, p. 38). A partial list of forty such books can be found in English (2008b, pp. 161–163) and includes such bestsellers as *Who Moved My Cheese?* by Spencer Johnson (1998); *Good to Great* by Jim Collins (2001); and the *Seven Habits of Highly Effective People* (1990) by Stephen Covey.

Under the category of "mystical metaphors" are words that Pattison avers stem from "apocalyptic, millenarian Christianity" and include "the language of visions, missions, doom scenarios" (p. 68), and harken to the earliest days of the Christian Church. Visions are not developed democratically, notes Pattison (1997); they are bestowed directly by God to prophets. The word "mission" is very much a term from the Christian past, where disciples were sent out to convince and persuade people to become Christians. Mormons still practice giving their young people "missions" before they reach adulthood. Pattison (1997) also is aware that in the past, when Christians practiced missions, it meant death to thousands of pagans.

Strategic planning with its visions and missions is a ritual. It often rests on visions and missions that have little to do with reality and are not open for challenge or change. By ritual, Pattison (2000) says he means, "activities that are symbolically important but that do not necessarily have the direct instrumental function that they may be assumed to have" (p. 179).

Pattison (1997) is especially critical of the idea of perfectionism in organizational life, where the slogans so often a part of TQM (total quality management), such as "get it right the first time every time," and that everyone should be treated "like a customer," are profoundly impossible. Says Pattison (2000), " ... the notion that individuals can have exactly what they want, when they want it, is profoundly false. No moral imperative in the natural order suggests that people should ... have constant access to an ever-available, inexhaustible supply of goodies" (p. 176).

We see the roots of religious values throughout the educational standards in the preparation of US school leaders. Known as the ISLLC Standards (Interstate Leadership Licensure Consortium), these benchmarks have been incorporated into licensure requirements and regional and national accreditation reviews. University courses must include the standards, and the activities and outcomes must be tracked through the curriculum.

Standard 1 indicates that "a school administrator is an educational leader who promotes the success of all students by facilitating the development, articulation, implementation, and stewardship of a vision of learning that is shared and supported by the school community" (Shipman, Queen, & Peel, 2007, p. 1). Here we have the educational leader functioning as a prophet. The standards indicate, "The school leader is the creator of the dream and the driving force that moves the dream forward" (Shipman, Queen, & Peel, 2007, p. 10). The educational leader does not work with colleagues to dream collectively, but "creates" the dream or vision alone, and the aim is pure perfection in that "all" students will experience success from this dream.

The idea of perfection and prophecy are intimately linked in the first standard for educational leaders. Schweitzer (1965) noted that, when Jesus and John the Baptist announced that the world was to be transformed because the Kingdom of God was near, "he called upon men to strive for perfection that would be required of them for participation in the new existence in a new world" (p. 15). We see the same sort of calling in the educational standards.

Once the prophecy is developed, just as in the analysis by Max Weber (1991/1922), the prophet's task is to direct and command obedience to the vision because it is a total system. The prophet expects compliance from all quarters to the totalizing image they created. In this case, teachers are not to question, but they must "examine current beliefs, develop a rationale for change, and consider new models and strategies for school improvement" (Shipman, Queen, & Peel, 2007, p. 11) because it is the "principal [who] determines the nonnegotiables—what must be part of the vision for the school to succeed. For example, you must ensure that the vision focuses on promoting success of all students" (Shipman, Queen, & Peel, 2007, p. 13). The rituals that accompany the creation of the vision are things such as

- collaboratively developing and implementing a shared vision (once the principal has created it),
- creating and implementing plans to achieve the goals,
- promoting continuous and sustainable improvement, and
- monitoring and evaluating progress and revising the plans.

Along with the idea of managerial perfection is the notion of progress in the concept of continuous improvement, which is unverifiable and rests on an act of faith. Even Edward Deming (1986), the father of TQM, once confessed, "A program of improvement sets off with enthusiasm, exhortations, revival meetings, posters, pledges. Quality becomes a religion" (pp. 322–323).

Much managerial activity is therefore outright religious in content, scope, and intensity. When concepts are imprecise and outcomes intangible and often elusive, there is no science of management in terms of valid and reliable functions. Instead, the goals and processes have been shorn of obvious religious titles and practices, but remain nevertheless though with secular names.

There are other unfortunate issues concerning religion in the schools to which we now turn.

WARRING METAPHORS

The metaphors of Biblical creation have left a deep imprint on the human psyche, despite the fact that Armstrong (2005) has pointed out that in the mythologies of the world, "a creation story never provided people with factual information about the origins of life" (p. 70). In 2009, the Texas Board of Education approved a science curriculum that permits teachers to introduce creationist perspectives contrasted to Darwin's theory of evolution (Simon, 2009a, p. A6). The Texas decision is financially lucrative, because that state is expected to spend approximately $600 million on science textbooks in the years ahead. Texas is one of twenty states that require local school districts to purchase only state-approved textbooks. It was this same

Board of Education that asked textbook publishers to delete "favorable references to Islam, discussions of global warming, and illustrations of breast and testicular self exams" (Simon, 2009a, p. A6).

There is a difference between a religious experience that opens a human being to the mysteries of the universe and one which erects dogma in the name of the infinite. Bertrand Russell (1986) wrote, "The soul of man is a strange mixture of God and brute, a battleground of two natures, the one particular, finite, self-centered, the other universal, infinite, and impartial" (p. 96). The impartial nature "leads to truth in thought, justice in action, and universal love in feeling" (p. 96), but the finite self, the brute self, "aims at dominion: it sees the world in concentric circles round the here and now, and itself as the God of that wished-for heaven" (p. 97).

THE POWER OF RELIGIOUS METAPHORS: THE UNIVERSAL VERSUS THE DOGMATIC AND PARTISAN EXPERIENCE

Religious metaphors are among the most powerful in the human experience and they will continue to be in the future for, as Pattison (1997) has acknowledged, they are "transformative and motivating" (p. 72) However, while we acknowledge religious metaphors' power, we do not view them as inerrant. Metaphors are polyvalent, especially those contained in Scripture. Scripture has been used by readers and leaders to justify slavery, persecution of the Jews, the accusation and execution of women as witches, the sanction and physical punishment of children, the assignment of guilt for disease, the mistrust and persecution of Catholics, and to prove that the earth is the center of the universe (see Hill & Cheadle, 1996). Scripture provides leaders with much metaphorical material for all kinds of uses.

As Howard Gardner (1995) has made us aware, leaders compete for followers by telling stories, and the most common stories are the ones most remembered. Within Western countries, stories from Scripture are often the ones most frequently employed because both leaders and followers know them. They provide the two-way traffic of communication and symbols in which leaders and followers move in a dynamic dyad. While we believe that one of the functions of leadership is to motivate and inspire, and to help people link organizational goals to their own and vice versa, we are extremely sensitive to the double-edged blade of religious metaphors in such pursuits.

Like all metaphors, scriptural metaphors come with historical baggage that may or may not always be apparent to the users. For this reason, one should be especially mindful of their origin. For example, saying "the handwriting is on the wall," which means a kind of warning that something ominous is going to occur, stems from the Old Testament Book of Daniel. At a feast when Belshazzar became the Babylonian king, a mysterious hand wrote a message on a palace wall announcing that his reign was numbered (Rogers, 1985, p. 121). Some people using this metaphor may be ignorant of its actual or literal derivation. Other metaphorical phrases with similar religious traces are "kill the fatted calf," which means get ready for a celebration and is from Luke 15:22, and a "thorn in the side," which refers to a painful annoyance and is taken from Corinthians 12:7 (see Rogers, 1985, pp. 148, 262).

Crossant (1994) points out the multiple meanings of these and other metaphors when discussing the Christian gospels. He notes that there are three layers present. The first is the "original situation"; that is, what actually happened. The second layer is the "transmissional" level, a tradition in which the actions reported in the first level are described or circumscribed in order to bring the person into line with prevailing legal or cultural norms of the day, or the norms of our own times. The third level is the "redactional" level, where certain facts are omitted or changed to support a line of argument or to make a point. When quoting scripture, many people do not know that the Bible was not originally written in English: The Old Testament was written in Hebrew and the New Testament in Greek (Funk, Hoover, & The Jesus Seminar, 1993, p. xvii). Modern historical research and scholarly opinion about the historical Jesus, for example, indicates that of the 1,500 sayings commonly attributed to Jesus, only about 20% were most likely actually spoken by him (Funk, Hoover, & The Jesus Seminar, 1993, p. 5). It should also be remembered that the time period from the death of Jesus to the first surviving gospels was approximately 175 years. To put that fact into perspective, a comparable time period would be from 1801, when in Britain Admiral Nelson defeated the Danes off Copenhagen and America when Thomas Jefferson was inaugurated as third President of the United States, to 1976 when Harold Wilson resigned as Prime Minister and Jimmy Carter was elected the 39th President (Grun, 1991). It is with this in mind that one must use metaphorical scripture with a good deal of caution, since meanings do change over time.

One good example is the oft-repeated metaphor of Adam and Eve and the serpent. As Frymer-Kensky (1996) points out, when this well-known story is read without "the prism of intervening interpretations . . . the biblical text is not so 'patriarchal' or misogynistic as we would otherwise have believed" (p. 1220). In the original text, Eve is not portrayed as a temptress or seductive. She speaks for the couple and presents logical reasons to the serpent. Neither is she singled out for special blame for their joint behavior; yet, in most images of Eve from this biblical portrait and in the popular mind, Eve represents primal disobedience for which not only was she punished, but all women were similarly impugned (Walker, 1983, pp. 288–291).

LEARNING HOW TO LEAD OUTSIDE THE COMMAND AND CONTROL MODEL

CONTEXT

Religion is important both literally and metaphorically in the context for educational leadership. Faith inspires and guides many in ways that will be discerned as positive or the opposite depending on one's viewpoint. Religion and spirituality have shaped education in profound ways throughout the world and over time. Equally, attitudes and rituals parallel to those inspired by religion are embedded in the warp and weft of educational practice. Most significantly, it is not the quest for improvement and for perfection that appears quasireligious in nature, but the fact that they no longer appear open to question. As goals, they have taken on the inviolacy of commandments and educational leaders are the priests.

LEADERSHIP PRACTICE

Perhaps the best exemplar of leadership practice with a religious bent is Robert Greenleaf's concept of *servant leadership* (Frick, 2004). Greenleaf was an anomaly in corporate America, a manager at AT&T (American Telephone and Telegraph), where he espoused a very different approach to leadership. Greenleaf noticed that "the best leaders and supervisors operated outside the traditional command-control model" (Greenleaf, 1935, as cited in Frick, 2004, p. 113), and he wrote that "no one should be made a supervisor to whom the workmen do not go for guidance and counsel before any designation of supervisory status is made" (Frick, 2004, p. 113). Greenleaf said that, if a leader is wise, "he knows how to drive hard with a light hand" and that "his organization will work with zeal and inspiration and never be conscious of his direction" (Greenleaf, 1935, as cited in Frick, 2004, p. 113).

Greenleaf developed his idea of leadership by insisting that one had to serve before one could lead—exactly the path modeled by Jesus. This perspective was not a "soft" model of management, but was extremely difficult to carry out in contemporary times, which were dominated by "Darwinian capitalism . . . or to disciples of the latest theories of leadership that use war, sports, and machines as their underlying metaphors" (Frick, 2004, p. 4). Such theories of leadership employed externals and a variety of forms of manipulation. Greenleaf's perspective was that one does not scramble over people or knock them down in advancing one's career, then decide to become benevolent once ensconced at the apex of the corporate hierarchy. A servant leader is not a "service provider," but a person who is deeply committed to "the growth of self, other people, institutions, and communities" (Frick, 2004, p. 5). A leader is first and foremost *a seeker*, not an achiever. Greenleaf's idea of leadership is that at a convention or a conference the true "boss" might be the last person one recognized as a leader in the traditional management mold. Today, the Greenleaf Center in Indianapolis, Indiana, carries on promoting his ideas since his death in 1990.

LEADERSHIP DEVELOPMENT NEEDS

Educational leaders have some of the same responsibilities as all of management, notably to secure the legitimacy and unity of the schools, agencies, and universities in which they work. Education is a moral enterprise connected to sets of values, and school leaders are the custodians of those values and moral purposes. We believe that the overt secular nature of education in most contemporary Western societies has blinded its leadership to the traditional religious thinking and rituals that are *sine qua non* of their continued effectiveness. Understanding that what leaders do is akin to what religious leaders do opens the door to a more realistic view of the nature of our work.

Concomitantly, there is great peril in espousing beliefs and practices that are little more than ideological ratio concatenations, which are largely symbolic and will actually have little to no effect on students or change how schools really work. We think that such things as strategic planning, visioning, and other trademarks of prophecy are symbolic acts and will have little to no effect on real improvement. We think that by identifying them simply as quasireligious rituals does not demean them, but places them in a more realistic framework, so that we can get on with doing those things that do make a difference. In this we were reminded by Burrows Dunham (1964) in his classic book, *Heroes and Heretics*, that " . . . the intellect is brief in attention, prone to illogic, and subvertible by prejudice. Thus we sometimes assert what we do not know, and we sometimes do not know what we assert" (p. 17).

Like Bertrand Russell's (1986) distinction between finite and infinite life, we see the continuing legacy of the infinite in embracing the purpose of education, that is, "truth in thought, justice in action, and universal love in feeling" (p. 96). Education is about transformation, a deep transformation that abolishes narrow categories and shallow distinctions. As nearly all of the great religions teach us, we are citizens of the world first, and Britons and Americans second. We all share the same planet, and if something happens to it we will all endure a common fate. As we are all born, so too must we all die, irrespective of our race, culture, language, preferred governmental institutions, or political philosophy. Whether we are in a pew somewhere in Christendom, a mosque in Istanbul, a synagogue in Jerusalem, an ashram in India or a monastery in Tibet, leaders see many paths to the infinite because "we are all children of God."

8

Leadership as Lunacy

The definition of insanity is doing the same thing over
and over again and expecting different results.

—Attributed to Albert Einstein

The adjective "lunatic" first appeared in English around 1300, bor-
rowed from the Old French word *lunatique* (insane), and traces its
etymological roots to the Latin *lunaticus*, meaning moonstruck. Formerly,
it was believed that attacks of insanity were precipitated by human reac-
tions to different phases of the moon (Barnhart, 1995, p. 446). More
recently, an external force inducing insanity is frequently understood to
be the organization in which a person works. The use of lunacy as a
metaphor to describe behaviors induced by organizations stretches back,
arguably, to Weber's nineteenth-century critique of the effect of bureaucracy on the human experience (Lassman & Spiers, 1994). Tod (1974)
writes of "administrative diseases." Caiden (1991) offers a list of 175
pathologies drawing on the analyses of numerous writers from 1949
onwards. The pathologies in question are self-destructive or organiza-
tionally destructive behavior.

This chapter examines leadership lunacy from two perspectives.
The first is an exploration of what appears to be rational behavior.
However, when it persists despite evidence to the decision maker that
his or her decisions aren't bringing about the desired outcomes, it

begins to resemble a kind of lunacy. Close up, behavior that seems eminently rational to the individual is actually irrational. We argue that persistent, irrational behavior is a form of insanity, even though the individual or individuals involved may not be psychiatrically certifiable as insane. A leader who consistently misreads data regarding the context in which the individual or group or country must function, or the negative outcomes of her or his choice and behavior is, in our opinion, a kind of lunatic. There is a failure to connect in a rational way with the context. The second approach examines leadership lunacy as a state of mind where work is enacted in ways that are dysfunctional. There is a fine line separating the two.

In relation to seemingly rational behaviors, one of the difficulties involved is that some forms of short-term behavior may look rational and sane, but prove to be the opposite when viewed over time. One thinks of US president Richard Nixon, who countenanced the Watergate break-in because he believed there was information that would reveal plots against him. From the beginning of the discovery of the break-in he lied about it until the end, when he was impeached. While Nixon's sanity was never seriously in question in psychiatric terms (though some non-experts called him paranoid), his repeated behavior before and during Watergate was insane. It disconnected from what was likely to and then what did happen. The opposite was the case with Akio Morita, the man who built Sony into an international giant. Morita contradicted what Japanese management was supposed to be all about. Instead of being a fan of consensus management, Morita was an autocrat. Early in his career, the Bulova watch company wanted to purchase 100,000 units of Sony's first transistor radio on the proviso they would put the Bulova name on the product. Morita declined the sale even after his superiors desired it. The unprecedented order was worth more than the company's total capitalization at the time. Morita wanted to build the Sony name into its own brand, instead of being a supplier to others. In retrospect, Morita said the decision was the best of his career (Nathan, 1999, p. A30). A "mad" decision, for example to lie or to turn down a great business offer, might be judged in retrospect as inspired. In these two cases, the individual felt that his actions were well justified by understanding the context and the probable consequence, but in only one case was this proved to be so. Nixon's actions were toxic.

LUNACY AS A FORM OF TOXICITY

One dimension of our concept of lunacy in leadership involves a leader who repeatedly makes bad judgments. Jean Lipman-Blumen (2005) has labeled such behaviors "toxic." Some of the behaviors she discusses are those that demean or demoralize followers; violate basic human rights;

propagate illusions; play to the most fundamental fears of followers; pit groups of followers against one another; use scapegoats; undermine aspects of the system in which they work that are designed to provide truth, justice, and excellence; engage in cronyism and corruption; and promote incompetence (pp. 19–20). We would add in this discussion regarding leadership lunacy the creation of an organizational culture that is corrupt, arrogant, and dishonest. Such behavior is lunatic because, ultimately, it is destructive not only of the very outcomes it is supposedly intended to achieve, but of individual lives and relationships.

The world had an unprecedented ringside seat to such lunatic behavior and its results in the crash of the business giants, huge banks, and corporations in the commercial world due to mismanagement, false assumptions, and greed in the first decade of the twenty-first century (Partnoy, 2003). Some of the first to fall were the leaders of Enron in the US, at the time the largest corporate bankruptcy in US history, from the seventh-largest corporation among the Fortune 500. The leadership of Enron was once branded as being led by "the smartest guys in the room." But as events eventually showed, the smartest guys in the room went to jail. As Fox (2003) notes in her history of Enron, sometime during 1996–1997 Enron crossed over from walking the line between the law and good accounting processes to outright fraudulent practices. Fox indicates that the top leadership of Enron either knew that the books were cooked or they were incompetent and did not know how to monitor the financial transactions of their own company. It doesn't really matter, but they were responsible for creating what everyone knew was a "corporate culture that valued aggression" and somewhere in that process it became acceptable to move away from looking at economic reality, as long as the existing accounting rules were followed (Fox, 2003, p. 308). Thus, an entire company with over 25,000 employees worldwide, valued at $100 billion in the stock market, went belly up. There was criminal behavior, but what made it also lunatic were its leaders ignoring reality, the cooked books, and the fictional financial security. Many crooks believe they can get away with their crimes, and some do. Lunacy is when a belief in getting away with it becomes a delusional escape from the real future, and yet no one ever accused Enron's corporate moguls, the board of directors, or the stockbrokers and other fiduciary wonks of being crazy.

In examining the fall of the international accounting firm, Arthur Andersen, Toffler (2003) refocused on the issue when she said "it's not the bad apples, it's the rotten culture" (p. 229). Toffler suggested that "more and more often, ingrained cultural practices—pressure to meet targets, implicit ways of dealing with clients, information and how it is used—shape the behaviour of more and more employees" (pp. 229–230). We proffer that leadership lunacy is not only about the psyche of individual leaders, but has to include the culture they establish in which other leaders and followers work. The culture of large urban school systems in the US is similar to some corporate lunacy cultures. For example, the Detroit, Michigan, public school system only graduates 24% of its students and has a long history of corruption. According to *The Wall Street Journal* (2009), school system audits in 2001 and 2004 showed that $2.5 million was misspent or unaccounted for and the city's school superintendent was fired for incompetence. In Washington, D.C., a school system in the nation's capital, only 60% of the students finish high school in four years. Only 6% of the system's sophomores read or do math on grade level (Fields, 2008, p. A6).

LEADERS AS LUNATICS

We have focused thus far on corporate and large-system lunacy where more than one person is responsible for the collective climate of a system. We next want to consider individual leaders and particularly educational leaders with policy responsibility. The first is that of William J. Bennett, who was President Reagan's secretary of education and President Bush's drug czar.

William Bennett is a conservative Republican orator and commentator on politics who has a long history of working with right-wing think tanks (Brock, 2005). He came to the US secretary of education position as the former chair of the National Endowment for the Humanities, where his agenda was "compatible with the White House's right wing" (Lugg, 2000, p. 172). He was of the opinion that money was not the answer for the problems of education. What schools required was "cultural literacy" and a return to classic works for the curriculum. He was an advocate of national testing and, as House (1998) observes, "Most reforms were designed to cost little new money . . . discipline students and teachers, and protect upper- and middle-class interests" (p. 21).

But somewhere in 2003 several national news magazines discovered that William J. Bennett was addicted to gambling, a discovery that was "certainly incongruent with the reputation of a man who preached self-control" (Turchiano, 2004, p. 27). There were tales that he lost more than $500,000 at the Bellagio in Las Vegas and $340,000 at Caesars in Atlantic City. When confronted with the incongruities of his behavior (a candidate for lunacy), Bennett said he gambled to relax.

The case of William J. Bennett, author of the best-selling *The Book of Virtues*, was the denial and hypocrisy of a man who preached moral values and condemned others for the flaws in their characters, while bellying up to the slot machines to "lose as much as $8 million as a result of his undisciplined behaviour in gambling halls" (Turchiano, 2004, p. 27). On Jean Lipman-Blumen's (2005) list of the attributes of toxic leaders we count among them, for William J. Bennett: lack of integrity, enormous ego, arrogance, amorality, and the reckless disregard for the costs of their actions.

THE LUNATIC PSYCHE

To take the second perspective on lunacy, we might follow an alternative approach by considering definitions of mental health. The World Health Organization defines health as "a state of complete physical, mental and social well-being and not merely the absence of disease or infirmity" (1946, p. 100). Sims (2003) notes laconically, "if total well-being is required perhaps virtually all of us are excluded" (p. 6). This chapter is not attempting to depict educational leaders as lunatics in a psychiatric, but rather a metaphorical, sense. A starting point is that schools are places of heightened psychic activity, "'emotional arenas,' in which individuals and groups deal daily with issues of anger, anxiety, disappointment, frustration, fear, guilt, love, friendship, and pleasure in highly context-specific and individual ways" (Blackmore, 2004, p. 444). Such intense relationships are overlaid on bureaucracy, which in itself is likely to induce pathologies (Caiden, 1991; Bozeman & Rainey, 1998). Beyond this, what is happening in our schools seems to be shifting the psyche. As Ball (2003) argues, standards and performativity-driven pressures change not just what we do as school leaders, but who we are. Current texts frequently employ lunacy metaphors to describe the effect. Jeffrey (2002), Ball (2003), and Blackmore (2004) all refer to the "schizophrenia" of the individual and the school. Ball charts "fantasy" and "alienation" (p. 222). Jeffrey refers to the "clinicalization of relations" (p. 541). Pathology, as a generic term for destructive behavior, appears repeatedly. Numerous writers are attempting to communicate what Blackmore calls the new "psychic economy," that is, schools as places of disturbed inner life and disordered relations with others (p. 440).

The behavior could be seen as revealing adjustment disorders: "*Adjustment disorders* involve distress and behavioral symptoms experienced in response to external stressors" (Kroska & Harkness, 2008, p. 195, original emphasis). It is not that administrators and faculty have, of themselves, adopted behaviors that reflect their individual life and choices; rather, Bozeman and Rainey (1998) argue that the fault, or that which induces pathological behavior, lies in the system. Faculty are exercising what they experience as an appropriate response to the daily stimuli in school or, as Ball (2003) puts it, "becoming *whatever it seems necessary to become*" (p. 225, original emphasis). Someone believing they are under attack from Martians may hit out, or hide behavior that is entirely appropriate to the scenario as they see it, but distinctly odd to those who do not perceive the same threat. In just such a way, school leaders may perceive behavior that seems counterproductive to others as a logical response to the pressures experienced in the working day.

SYMPTOMS, SIGNS, AND PATHOLOGIES

We will explore in more detail the metaphorical world—the similarities and dissimilarities of lunacy and leadership in early twenty-first-century schools—to illuminate how the system appears to be pathologizing leaders' behavior. Clinical medicine distinguishes symptoms and signs of psychopathology (Sims, 2003). Symptoms are the perceptions of the individual, how he or she feels, what each reports he or she is experiencing. Signs are physical manifestations that can be verified by use of observation or touch or other diagnostic procedures giving a reliable result. Drawing on the metaphorical analyses of current pathologies of administration, we proffer some ideas on the symptoms and signs evident in our schools of delusion, psychopathy, disconnected relationships, and obsessive–compulsive behavior.

Delusions

According to Sims (2003), "a delusion is a false, unshakeable idea or belief . . . it is held with extraordinary conviction and subjective certainty (p. 117). The key elements of delusion are the strength of belief with which an idea is held, its patent falseness to all but the deluded, and the fact that no amount of logic can dislodge it (Jaspers, 1963). Delusions are apparent to anyone but the individual concerned. As Sims (2003) puts it: "Very rarely does anyone claim to be deluded" (p. 117).

Greenberg (1999) pinpoints one delusion shared by policy makers, governors, and principals alike, that the range of activities and outcomes demanded by policy makers, parents, and the wider community is achievable only if principals and supervisors of high caliber can be recruited, trained adequately, and perform to specification. So, for example, failure to halt millennia of education further embedding the advantage and disadvantage of families is the result of leaders' inability to assure adequate teaching. The assumption is widespread that principals can act heroically to enact a wide range of roles to reengineer society. The superman metaphor is used frequently, implying that principals will not only take on an unrealistically demanding task, but will embrace the role and its demands, and be seen to be enjoying it (Jones, 1999, p. 447).

In a survey in England, one principal of a school for children with special learning needs characterized the role of principal as, "All things to all men! Or bloody near impossible—take your pick" (National Union of Teachers, 2006). The principal goes on to add, "Mind you I thoroughly enjoy the challenge of the job." Similarly, in an exploration of metaphors used to describe principals in Slovenia, Trnavčevič & Vaupot (2009) identify a wide range of assumed roles including "metaphors, such as 'magician,' 'superman' and 'man of authority'" (p. 98). The metaphors of superman and magician embody the expectation that the principal will achieve the impossible; that principals can both enact a very wide and diverse range of roles, and do "everything no one else is prepared to do, or hasn't done well." (NUT, 2006, para. 17). Principals are also expected to be a "Jack of all trades! Educator, manager, financial wizard, social worker, Government dogsbody" (NUT, 2006, para. 17), as well as being held responsible for all failings: "The person blamed for everything from standards to crumbling buildings" (NUT, 2006, para. 17).

The policy makers who enact legislation and shape principals' preparation programs hold the delusional belief most strongly; they regularly excoriate administrators' performance as the root of the failure to achieve higher standards for all children ("Remove Bad Teachers," 2007). Incompetent or underperforming teachers are regularly criticized as a key element related to failing children. By extension, principals are incompetent for failing to deal with the situation. A key advisor to the British government, Sir Cyril Taylor, was reported as saying "there were about 17,000 'poor' teachers in England. They were unable to control classes and were damaging the education of about 400,000 children" ("Remove Bad Teachers," 2007, para. 2). This was linked to the outcome of "400,000 of our children attending low-attaining schools; 75,000 leave schools at 16 with hardly any qualifications at all; five million adults are functionally illiterate"(para. 6). He called on head teachers to be stronger in getting rid of poor performers, saying, "the head teacher that is good can take the necessary action, you get the wrong people off the bus and get the right people on the bus in the right seats" ("Remove Bad Teachers," 2007, para. 7). Such views are regularly reported from a range of sources, though not all are so explicit. The delusion is ubiquitous, that "good" principals could solve the fundamental problems of education if they acted rightly.

Some principals refute this; their argument, based on much evidence, points out the many other factors at play. This does not shake governments' belief that schools and principals hold responsibility for failure. Some principals enter the delusional world, relishing the heroic status applied and the triumph of managing an unmanageable workload and expectations. They share the delusion and embrace the "hero" role, put a positive spin on all eventualities and show no weakness to faculty, parents, or inspectors. The example of a few principals who "turn around" failing schools is held as the standard that all can attain whatever the context. Such a belief matches the three criteria of delusions: it is strongly held, and there is overwhelming evidence that it is false. Nevertheless, logic does not shake it.

If policy makers are the primary holders of the delusion that principals can act as superman or magician, principals are the primary holders of a complementary delusion that they are benign and work selflessly for the best interests of all students. There is overwhelming research evidence that this is not the case (Lumby, 2006; Reay, 2001). Both government and principals employ "active denial" of the complex human and societal factors that render schools places of failure and unhappiness for many children (Araújo, 2005; Carter & Osler, 2000; Lumby & Morrison, 2009; Slee, 1994) and cling to delusions that offer a more comfortable psychic position than facing the evidence that principals may act in ways that are morally dubious and conscienceless, metaphorically as psychopaths.

Psychopathy

Psychopathy is a widely recognized term. Hamilton (2008) depicts its use as describing "instrumentally impulsive individuals with poor behavioral controls who callously and remorselessly bleed others for purely selfish reasons via manipulation, intimidation, and violence" (p. 232). Hamilton adds, "psychopathy does not present as subjective discomfort or self-reported disease; psychopaths usually have a sense of ease—sometimes gallingly robust—about their way of being, and it is from wounded others that complaints arise" (p. 232). So principals would not see themselves, even metaphorically, as psychopaths. Others might recognize some similarities.

We focus here on two ways in which conscienceless behavior is evident and its connection to the advent of new systems within schools; the selection of students and the provision of information to allow students to make choices. Both areas of behavior are related to school markets or marketization (Gibson & Asthana, 2000). The kind of competition that has always been a driving force in business and industry has been fostered in schools in the UK and the US since the late twentieth century. A raft of policy is responsible, such as site-based management, which gives principals more autonomy to act competitively; the publication of examination results, fostering comparisons between schools; and financial systems that reward the recruitment and retention of students. Schools do not sell products in competition with others to achieve a profit, but West & Pennell (2007) believe that there is competition between educational providers, just as there is within conventional markets: "In the case of schools there is therefore competition between the institutions for 'customers' (that is, pupils or their proxies, their parents)" (p. 207). There is widespread evidence that this has led to, in the title of Coates and Adnett's (2002) article, "cream-skimming and dreg-siphoning." The cream are students who are well behaved and of high prior academic and/or sporting attainment. The dregs are those students who are "less desirable . . . low achieving, with special educational needs or disaffected" (p. 220). That many school principals covertly select students, excluding those who are viewed as less desirable, has been of concern to the British government for some time. Bush, Coleman, and Glover (1993) found that a third of their sample of secondary schools was using interviews to discriminate against some students and families. The use of interviews to select students, particularly by faith-based schools, has persisted as a point of contention, as has the selection of students by attributes for specialist schools in England.

It would seem that principals and governors manipulate admission criteria to ensure that they maintain the advantage of prestige and high attainment results while avoiding the inconvenience of students who may be demanding because of their special needs, or previous or anticipated behavior (Archer & Fletcher-Campbell, 2005; Gewirtz, Ball, & Bowe, 1995; Thrupp, 1999). Not all schools and school leaders behave in this way, but it would seem that a substantial proportion does. As one of a suite of behaviors related to the orientation that thinks "I will do anything I have to, to save my school" (Blackmore, 2004, p. 542), and not just to survive but to maintain or increase status, principals are willing to set aside the needs of children in their local community in order to maximize advantage to their school. Is this not indeed the action of a "conscienceless individual" (Hamilton, 2008, p. 232)? Of course, such actions are not new. Elite schools have been selecting pupils for centuries. What has changed is that such elitist and exclusionary attitudes have spread far more widely to the neighborhood school.

There is evidence of a persistent pattern in England since the early 1990s of schools adjusting admission policies to their advantage and governments responding with legislation or codes of practice to try to deter discriminatory practice (West & Pennel, 2007). Ironically, government established the market system, while at the same time it attempts to control the resulting negative effects of competitive behavior. Aggressively competitive behavior is seen as acceptable in business and industry, or at least it was until the credit crunch of 2008. Bakan (2004) argues that in business the psychopathic, conscienceless individual is part of a system that views it as acceptable to set aside conscience and morality. As Hamilton (2008) describes, "one must discern a predatory and poisonous chameleon against a background that is, distressingly, itself a kind of predatory and poisonous chameleon" (p. 238). Similarly, in schools, principals and governors who manipulate the system to their advantage at the cost of children, families, and communities are part of a market system based on commercial values that reflect the psychopathic tendencies of the corporate world.

Just as the choice of children and parents to enter a school may be thwarted by conscienceless behavior, so the choice of exit may be ruthlessly manipulated. There is evidence of schools withholding full information from young people on their options for continuing their post-compulsory education when the information might lead to an exit and, with the exit, loss of funds (Gorard et al., 2009; Keys et al., 1998). The psychopath of literature and film is a monstrous figure, violent, singular, and an anomaly among humanity. The corporate psychopath is indistinguishable from the crowd: ordinary, accepted, acting through legal means. So too, metaphorically, some school leaders may be acting in a way that puts self-interest first and lacks conscience: not the extraordinary monster of fiction, but ordinary. In Ball's (2003) phrase, within the pressured, standards-driven, competitive system, they have become what "*it seems necessary to become*" (p. 225, original emphasis). Their professional relations with others have become disordered, with a disconnection from children and faculty.

Disconnections

Edward and Munro (2008) suggest that "a sense of disconnectedness from others" (p. 605) is a symptom of depression. Disconnections in relationships are noted frequently in the education literature; that is, a breakdown in mutually supportive relations between administrators and faculty, between faculty members and, most disturbingly, between faculty and children. A further disconnection is between administrators and faculty members and their work. As long ago as 1978, Forsyth and Hoy found evidence of educators who "experience work as lacking intrinsic meaning or value" (p. 91) as a result of alienation. The frequency of reference to disconnection and alienation in the literature of the twenty-first century suggests that the incidence and intensity may have increased. The related terms "alienation" and "disconnection" have been used variously in sociology and political science over time. Though Forsyth and Hoy (1978) suggest that the use of alienation as synonymous with a belief that "something important has been lost" (p. 80) is rather inexact, such a general feeling accords exactly with a depressive symptom. Exploring the metaphor's potential similarities to administration, it might be useful to distinguish disconnection as a sense that there is no relationship where a relationship previously existed or was expected, and alienation as a sense of negative relations, of divergence from or distaste for the interests, values, or activity of others. Following the metaphor further, just as the response to depression might be to try to understand the cause, so Forsyth and Hoy (1978) suggest that it is incumbent on those who study educational administration to explore "the relationships between subjective states and their objective social roots" (p. 81). A few administrators may be clinically depressed. It is not they who are the focus here, but the very large number who appear to be experiencing disconnection and alienation, the metaphoric symptoms of depression.

The relationship between senior administrators and faculty seems to be undergoing a sea change. Various concepts have been used to analyze the nature and causes of changed relations: managerialism (Elliott & Crossley, 1997; Randle & Brady, 1997), performativity (Ball, 2003; Hartley, 2007), and new public management (Deem, 1998). Randle and Brady suggest that managerialism emerged as a concept in the UK in the early 1980s (Farnham & Horton, 1993; Flynn, 1993; Pollitt, 1990) and it consists of a package of management ideas, techniques and styles including ℯ strict financial management and devolved budgetary controls;

ℯ the efficient use of resources and an emphasis on productivity;

ℯ the extensive use of quantitative performance indicators;

ℯ the development of consumerism and the discipline of the market;

ℯ the manifestation of consumer charters as mechanisms for accountability;

ℯ the creation of a flexible workforce, using flexible/individualized contracts, appraisal systems, and performance related pay; and

ℯ the assertion of "the managers' right to manage." (Randle & Brady, 1997, p. 230)

The final bullet signals the key change in relationships; managers are asserting a right to decide and to direct, replacing previous norms of collegiality.

Performativity is a related term depicting the environment that both prefigures and results from managerialist action (Olssen & Peters, 2005; Steer et al., 2007). Deem (1998) suggests that the performative environment is evident in

the use of internal cost centres, the fostering of competition between employees, the marketisation of public sector services and the monitoring of efficiency and effectiveness through measurement of outcomes and individual staff performances. (pp. 49–50)

Performativity conceptualizes the systems, and managerialism the actions within.

While tight direction and surveillance of staff, competition rather than collaboration, and stringent accountability may be evident in bureaucracies stretching back for centuries (Samier & Lumby, 2010), the more technologically developed means for monitoring performance and publishing results to a wider public gaze has metamorphosed the environment into one in which control may seriously distort behavior. In a study of the impact of performativity on staff relations in the UK, Jeffrey (2002) quotes Toni, a deputy head and so a senior administrator, who says,

I have become less sympathetic. I now identify less with those who don't fit this system. They know what the game is and they should be fulfilling what we, as a school, ask of them, because there is no place for them otherwise. You can't be an individual in this system at the moment, it just makes it hard work for everybody if you try to be. (p. 537)

Jeffrey (2002) concludes that previous values that put people and caring for each other at the heart had been "significantly affected by the introduction of the performativity environment" (p. 532). Not only are senior leaders aware of their changed attitudes to faculty, teachers also feel the effects of a changed relationship:

> The head was very, very unsympathetic when my daughter was rushed back into hospital. One of the reasons why I decided to come here was the humanity she showed. Before the pressure of the Ofsted inspection I don't think she would have reacted in that way. It's affected my view of her as a manager. (p. 540)

and

> Not only did I have pressure to return to work after the death of my mother, but I was threatened with loss of salary if I didn't return quickly. I was looked upon as part of this machinery. The head actually said to me that I am very highly thought of, and that a significant part of the machine was missing and it had to be put back. (p. 540)

The use of the machine metaphor points up the absence of humanist values and the resulting disconnection (the absence of warm relations between head teacher or deputy and faculty) and alienation (disgust at the values in play). Such experience is also evident in relations between faculty and in faculty relations with children. Consider the report of a teacher in Jeffrey's study (2002), who says, "I'm working *at* the children and it's not a very pleasant experience. There is this feeling of being alienated from it all, divorced from it all" (p. 536, original emphasis).

A similar orientation to children is reported from Australian principals. Blackmore (2004) depicts some as driven to a willingness to act to the detriment of children if necessary, reporting, "they stamp on us so we stamp on kids" (p. 453). In the same way as faculty, children have become objects, units in a system where some leaders are driven to act without care and sensitivity, prioritizing the fulfillment of prescribed outcomes, however meaningless or crushing to others. It is not suggested that all principals and faculty act in this way; rather, the research suggests that such disconnected and alienated relations are widespread and connected to the changing context within which schools function.

Goldstein and Rosselli (2003) point out that there are numerous potential causes of depression: psychological, environmental, and biological. Similarly, following through with the metaphor, the disconnection and alienation in schools, if viewed as a symptom of a particular condition, may have multiple and complex roots. However, two phenomena stand out as particularly responsible: demands to conform to policy-dictated procedures and standards, and ongoing high levels of surveillance. The propensity of organizations to induce pathology is long established. Caiden (1991) makes it clear that pathological behavior is "not the individual failings of individuals who compose organizations but the systematic shortcomings of organizations" (p. 490). As the demands of organizations intensify, the humanity of workers and humanistic values are threatened. Forsyth and Hoy (1978) remind us that "hyperconformity to group norms is the source of Marxian alienation" (p. 80). Curricula, attainment expectations, inspection, and accountability requirements are detailed in ways that increasingly deny freedom of choice and action to educators. Their work is increasingly objectified and human relations follow suit.

Following the "war on terror," a worldwide debate has considered the justification for surveillance on those suspected of posing a threat. No such intense debate has taken place in relation to the surveillance of those who work in our public services and who face "the terrors of performativity" (Ball, 2003, p. 216). Blackmore (2004) reports "the need to be visibly and constantly performing" (p. 450). Ongoing observation of lessons, league tables of results, and inspection systems all intrude their gaze. Increasingly, there is no part of a school's work that cannot be viewed by those external to the organization. Some might argue that this is right and proper when it is the well-being of children that is at stake. However, even animals in zoos are provided with a reliable place of retreat from the public gaze. Not so the work of schools. Just as animals subject to the strain of constant view begin to display behavior indicative of stress, so principals and faculty offer evidence of disrupted and alienated relations and values.

Obsessive–Compulsive Behavior

Abramowitz, Whiteside, and Deacon (2005) describe obsessive–compulsive disorder (OCD) as "an anxiety disorder that involves (a) intrusive unwanted thoughts, ideas, or images that evoke anxiety (obsessions), and (b) behavioral or mental rituals performed to neutralize this distress (compulsions)" (p. 56). The trigger for obsessive–compulsive symptoms in educators appears to be what Ball terms "the new management panopticism" (p. 219) leading to "high levels of existential anxiety and dread" (p. 219). The environment is well captured by Ball:

> The teacher, researcher, academic are subject to a myriad of judgments, measures, comparisons and targets. . . . A sense of being constantly judged in different ways, by different means, according to different criteria, through different agents and agencies. There is a flow of changing demands, expectations and indicators that makes one continually accountable and constantly recorded. We become ontologically insecure: unsure whether we are doing enough, doing the right thing, doing as much as others, or as well as others, constantly looking to improve, to be better, to be excellent. And yet it is not always very clear what is expected. (p. 220)

Not surprisingly, given this context, the word "obsessive" or "obsession" appears frequently in relation to educational leadership, particularly in discussions of standards or quality in schools (Aun, Riley, Atputhasamy, & Subramaniam, 2006; Bharwani, 2006; Ng, 2007). Obsessive behavior is discerned not just in school leaders, but in parents and students. The obsessive preoccupation with results spreads like a disease from faculty to children. In a study of Singapore schools, a student comments, "the trouble is not with the teachers and the principal. I mean teachers and principals all have this obsession with results. But if you look at some of your own friends, they are worse" (Ng, 2004, p. 87).

Anxiety about not achieving good enough results, or results sufficient to win whatever competition is in train with other schools, leads to a variety of compulsive behaviors. Three areas are explored here: the use of information technology, demands for compliance, and the increasing intensification of work.

The intrusion of information technology into all aspects of working life has fueled a rise in the compulsive collection and dissemination of data (Porter & Kakabadse, 2006). Boyle (2001) depicts the obsessive–compulsive behavior of how "we take our collective pulse 24 hours per day with the use of statistics." Leney, Lucas, and Taubaum (1998) give the example of a college that submits one-and-a-half-million pieces of data to the administration three times a year, and has the information returned with the explanation that there was an error in two records. Ever more finely-grained data concerning student performance, department performance, faculty performance, and school performance demand the collection of immense amounts of figures, the utility of which are subject to fierce debate. For example, systems of calculating value-added attainment, despite ongoing and sometimes rancorous challenge as to their validity, are used for all schools in England. Yet many faculty (and parents) do not fully understand the detail of calculations or use the results in any meaningful way (Sparkes, 1999). The obsession with statistics, or at least numbers, leads to compulsive ritual compilation of variants on themes of student profile, attendance, performance, and outcomes. Any aspect of school activity is rendered impotent if not supported by a related set of figures. While the feeling of insecurity may be a symptom, the huge amounts of statistical and other data swirling round the system is a physical sign of lunacy.

In symbiosis with the obsessive–compulsive manipulation of figures is an intensifying need for compliance. Hood (1995) notes that anxiety attracts "predator interests," which are nourished by demanding ever more detailed verbal and written accounts of actions and outcomes (p. 95). Blackmore (2004) charts the path toward obsessive–compulsive behavior amongst school leaders:

Once one becomes active in the game of performativity, then the performances are repeated until they become internalized.

Thus the external processes of regulation of the disciplinary technologies, the symbolic, becomes naturalized, part of the taken-for granted, part of the language and landscape of education. (p. 455)

The rituals that are demanded by legislation, by policy, and by public expectation become so habituated that their absence would cause anxiety. Anxiety leads to an intense need to allay such feelings by repetition of what has been performed before. Deviation causes unease. Leaders demand compliance with standards in order to maintain a fragile sense of control. Bozeman and Rainey (1998) suggest that leaders have always had a need for control to some degree. The performativity environment has exacerbated such tendencies, leading to the disconnected and compulsive compliancy behaviors reported in Jeffrey's study (2002).

Achieving exact compliance demands a good deal from "greedy work" (Gronn, 2003, p. 147). The third compulsion is therefore the need to keep working, to work for ever more hours each day and to feel unease if this pattern is broken as part of the twenty-four-seven culture, and "perpetual urgency" (Porter & Kakabadse, 2006, p. 538). A compulsion is evident when individuals feel the need to keep working, even when the working day has ended or they are in leisure time at weekends or vacations. Porter and Kakabadse's (2006) study of corporate and public-sector workers found evidence of pressures that are familiar to all educators, including, "information overload (e-mail, corporate websites), responding in near-real time, extended working hours through technology, encroachment of work into discretionary time and multi-tasking" (p. 540). The root compulsion, that is "intrusive unwanted thoughts" (Abramowitz, Whiteside, & Deacon, 2005, p. 56) was clear. One manager explained the symptom, saying,

> I have employees who, if they leave at 5 or 6 o'clock they feel guilty. It's not the norm for them to leave at 5 or 6, but they'll say, "Well I have a doctor's appointment or today was a tough day, and I'm going to leave early." Why do we feel that way? Why do we feel guilty leaving, basically, on time? (Porter & Kakabadse, 2006, p. 549)

The compulsion "rituals performed to neutralize this distress" (Abramowitz et al., 2005, p. 56) is, among many others, not to arrive or leave on time. The manager's further explanation makes the compulsive nature clear: "It's accepted and people buy into it, because they don't feel they have a choice" (Porter & Kakabadse, 2006, p. 549). Schools become places of mass organizational obsession and compulsion, yet because those outside the school may share the madness, or at least see it as a norm, lunacy prevails.

THE LUNACY METAPHOR

CONTEXT

At time of writing, there is renewed emphasis on sanity and ethics in the corporate world. Bakan (2004) depicts societal expectations: "corporations are now often expected to deliver the good, not just the goods; to pursue values, not just value, and to help make the world a better place" (p. 29). This has always been the task of education and yet, ironically, as corporations move, at least in public rhetoric, toward values-driven practices, the mores of competition and self-interest burgeon in our schools. Education has to some degree exchanged position with business. Values are set aside to deliver primarily the economic goods, rather than the social good. The psychic fracture induced reveals itself in the lunatic behaviors outlined in this chapter. Nietzsche (2008) asserted that lunacy was relatively rare in individuals but pretty much the norm among groups and nations. We have shown that to be the case when considering organizational lunacy.

LEADERSHIP PRACTICE

The metaphor of lunacy has uncovered startling similarities between behaviors that might in other contexts be diagnosed as symptomatic of mental illness, and the behavior of leaders and others in our schools and corporations. MacIntyre (1981) suggested, "we have—very largely, if not entirely—lost our comprehension, both theoretical and practical, of morality" (p. 239). Our exploration of the metaphor of lunacy in relation to school leadership reminds us that sanity is in part predicated on psychic confidence, a sense of acting rightly. Our analysis indicates strongly the interplay of lost moral purpose and lost mental balance.

Unfortunately, the sense of lost moral purpose is pervasive in our times, although there is much chest-beating and editorial moralizing about what principles and values beyond greed should be at work in the market place. In the continuing wake of the financial market meltdown all over the world in the first decade of the twenty-first century, the corporate culture that has emphasized personal aggrandizement as the best basis for a healthy economy has vividly shown its impropriety, especially for those organizations rendering a public service such as schools and colleges. The reinvestment of public morality in essential social services such as education may be the revitalizing force that ultimately re-establishes the credibility not only of education but of all those who are educated and go on to work in the private sector.

LEADERSHIP DEVELOPMENT NEEDS

The chapter has explored how the pressures of the organization and of wider social systems induce states of mind and behaviors that are irrational. Leaders do not usually choose to exhibit lunatic behavior. The latter is an adaptation in response to cultural expectations and stress. Leadership preparation and development to resist such adaptation is problematic. How does development nurture resilience sufficient to protect moral standards and rationality? Resilience is defined by Giles (2006) as "an individual's effort to not only withdraw from or shield against unwanted change, but to adapt and assert one's own identity and purposes over and against change" (p. 181). She concludes that we do not know enough about how development might initiate or sustain the ability to be resilient. Many programs currently seem designed to propel leaders toward lunacy, obsession with data, compulsive working hours, a delusional heroic stance, and the irrational repetition of ineffective tactics. Restoring sanity is an urgent need.

9

Metaphors of Leadership

> If thought corrupts language, language can also corrupt thought.
>
> —Orwell (1946/1961, p. 364)

When we hear the phrase "once upon a time," we know that what follows is a fabrication, a story, a tale of something that has not happened. Yet we also believe that the tale may communicate profound truths, and that the story is in some sense about what has happened and will happen. The Arabic version of the beginning of a story, "It was so and not so," captures perfectly that liminal state where we both disbelieve and believe (Anderson, 2005, p. 591). The previous chapters have explored the power of metaphors to create that state of belief where we both know that it is not so, that school administrators are not, for example, lunatics, machines, or warriors, and yet in some sense we know it is so; we understand that some administrators may have, in some sense, become such or at least adopted such an outlook or perspective about themselves, the schools they lead, and the teachers and students with whom they interact. In this sense, the metaphors leaders use to describe themselves and their work represent an explanation, a kind of classification and a prejudice; that is, a preferred way or manner of going about thinking about what they do. One of the reasons for writing this book was to expose these metaphors as connectors to larger and more complex patterns of thought, many with historical traces to practices that are not immediately obvious or always understood, and to sketch out the implications of their continued usage in the field of education. In this sense, metaphors both reveal and conceal. They are thoughts and unthoughts, like two sides of the same coin.

THE USES OF METAPHORS

If metaphors create a cognitive state where something both is and is not, they may have the power both positively to create belief and commitment to an idea or a practice and negatively to bamboozle receivers into a false position or poor or even detrimental practice. We begin with the power of language, and specifically of metaphors, to bamboozle.

In 1946, Orwell exclaimed that struggling against the abuse of language was deplored by many as Luddite, a futile attempt to hold back the torrent that is ever-changing language. He nevertheless believed that it was important to resist and suggested that a decline in language has political and economic causes. If stated intentions are of dubious morality, language is a ready tool for "the defense of the indefensible" (Orwell, 1946/1961, p. 362). The basis of such use or abuse of language is a symbiotic relationship between slovenly language and slovenly thought. He analyzed forms of language that depress rather than stimulate thought. For example, pretentious diction might disguise oppressive actions, or meaningless words may skitter across the mind, blocking out any real engagement with ideas. Dead metaphors are especially identified as those that have lost all power to stimulate thought and may act as a substitute for thinking. We may no longer process the similarities and dissimilarities of a dead metaphor to reach new insights. Rather, the dead hand of the metaphor provokes cognitive skipping; we skip that bit, accept it without assessing whether we ought, and carry on. Dead metaphors may become clichés such as "fiddling while Rome burns," "the calm before the storm" or, as we have seen in the sports chapter, a "sticky wicket." In education, when we use the dead metaphor "delivery," for example, we no longer think about what is implied by using such a mechanistic term in relation to something as fluid and complex as learning. Well-worn phrases and metaphors fill the gap where there might otherwise be real thinking, both requiring and reflecting a careful choice of words, so metaphors fill silence with noise but repress thought and communication. Administrators, students, and parents become cotton wool recipients of language, absorbing what is said or written and in the process becoming less than themselves, soggy and superficial in their thoughts.

As well as repressing thought, metaphors may also disguise or misdirect. Orwell (1946/1961) stated, "When there is a gap between one's real and one's declared aims, one turns as it were instinctively to long words and exhausted ideas" (p. 364). In the UK Department for Children, Schools and Families Annual Report (DCSF, 2009b), the Minister for Education declares the "the aim of putting young people and children at the heart of everything [they] do" (p. 3). The metaphor of the heart, with its association of love and centrality to life, diverts attention from thinking about the many other documents emanating from government that put economic competition as the primary driver of education plans (HM Treasury, 2006). Here, the heart appears connected to the wallet, not the emotion of love.

Poletti (2004), writing fifty years after Orwell, reprises the analysis of language to uncover the range of ends served. She suggests that metaphors can entrench positions and stifle debate, manage resolution of contradictory experiences, manage conflicts, create tolerance of ambiguity, set limits to debate, deflect challenge, and manipulate emotion. For her they are both "performative" and "persuasive" (p. 268). Examples from the discourse related to education come readily to hand. David Cameron was leader of the Conservative Party in 2009 and therefore of the then Government Opposition in the UK. He became Prime Minister in 2010. In his speech to the Conservatives at the close of their annual conference, he painted a black picture of the state of the nation, but suggested that, under a Conservative government, "Yes, there is a steep climb ahead. But I tell you this, the view from the summit will be worth it" (Cameron, 2009, para. 3). This widely reported metaphor performs several of the functions that Poletti (2004) identified. For many years, the UK government has stressed the resources and attention given to improving education. Despite this, many families experience schooling for their children as a repetition of their own negative experience, resulting in a sense of failure and exclusion rather than success and empowerment (Lumby & Morrison, 2009). The picture of constant improvement often painted by administrators in the school and policy makers at national level is belied by the experience of the children (Lumby, 2007). Cameron's metaphor reconciles these contradictory experiences. It may be tough and bleak on the mountainside, but that is because we are not yet at the summit. If we just keep climbing, it will be difficult, but worth it. The view will be great. The implication is that what is lacking is the will of the people; the effort of the people. They have not yet climbed far enough. The dislocation between what is usually communicated—achievement and progress— and what is actually experienced—lack of progress—is reconciled. The debate here is not about, for example, how education is structured, how the National Curriculum functions, or how principals compete against each other to get the "best" students and exclude the "challenging." Rather, the debate is about persistence on a difficult pathway that is always going upwards, the latter a universal signifier of progress. If there is challenge to the policies outlined, it can be defused as somehow not legitimate; resistance equates to not struggling to keep going and to not accepting the struggle as justified. Limits are set to the debate. The current state of affairs is not about the detail of policy choices, but about accepting leadership though challenging times. Emotions are manipulated. The metaphor imports the sense of achievement, well-being, and awe that many have experienced as they climb to a viewpoint and see wonders spread out before them.

What, then, are the actual polices that will achieve this? If one examines the suggested actions of a Conservative government at the same convention (Gove, 2009), they include developing "a Troops to Teachers program—to get professionals in the army who know how to train young men and women into the classroom" (para. 64). On the one hand, a tempting emotional call to climb a mountain; on the other, importing soldiers into classrooms to instill discipline. The metaphor Cameron used is dangerously seductive, beguiling citizens to ignore the actual plans and feel the emotion instead. It encourages them to locate responsibility for failure in insufficient effort and persistence. It provides a goal that is nebulous, and reachable because so undefined. It holds out a dream, not a strategy.

Similar tactics are in evidence if one turns to a speech on education by President Obama in the US (Obama, 2009). Obama uses the same metaphor of climbing, stating, "our children should climb higher than we did" (para. 10) but also incorporates the extended metaphor of a race: "we've let . . . other nations outpace us" (para. 11), and "we will end what has become a race to the bottom in our schools and instead spur a race to the top" (para. 20). Education is framed as both a competition with other nations and as internal competition between students to succeed or to decline further. Just as Cameron held out a dream scenario, so Obama explicitly invokes the American dream of raising oneself through sheer effort. He speaks of "a dream shared by all Americans. It's the founding promise of our nation: That we can make of our lives what we will; that all things are possible for all people; and that here in America, our best days lie ahead" (para. 52). Just as Cameron called people to a difficult pathway where effort will bring rewards, so Obama places responsibility for success with individuals and families:

> No government policy will make any difference unless we also hold ourselves more accountable as parents—because government, no matter how wise or efficient, cannot turn off the TV or put away the video games. Teachers, no matter how dedicated or effective, cannot make sure your child leaves for school on time and does their homework when they get back at night. These are things only a parent can do. These are things that our parents must do. (para. 47)

Students, too, must try, as Obama states, "it's the responsibility of our students to walk through the doors of opportunity" (para. 54).

Both Cameron and Obama were using metaphors to support a grand educational narrative—that of universal success. They imply through metaphors of races, of climbs, of going through doors, that the means for every student to become successful is within their hands and those of their family. They use language to sucker the public into believing that, if things are not right in schools, then the blame can be apportioned not to poverty or racism, or the self-protection and aggrandizement of the advantaged, or to government policies, but to personal failure. There is no doubt that individuals, both parents and students, must bear some responsibility for their education and its results, but the use of the metaphors explored briefly here directs attention to this aspect of education and no other. It is a false communication. There are, of course, policy details elsewhere in both speeches—plans for action—usually in general terms. For example, in Obama's (2009) case, "doing more for children with special needs" (para. 17) and in Cameron's, "Discipline. Setting by ability. Regular sport" (para. 8). However, it is the metaphors that hit home and the metaphors that are more widely reported and remembered.

Metaphors are used to attack the preparation of administrators and teachers also. The Obama Administration US secretary of education, Arne Duncan, criticized schools of education for doing a mediocre job of preparing teachers, using the metaphor of the "Bermuda triangle" to liken the situation to when students "sail in, but no one knows what happens to them after they come out" (Sawchuk, 2009, p. 12). He called these programs "cash cows" (see Spears, 1997, p. 63), because they required less support than the more prestigious programs in the arts and sciences and were a steady source of income to keep enrollments small in those academic areas, at the expense of quality in teacher education. The criticisms are vague and unsubstantiated, but again metaphors prove a ready tool to induce unease.

GRAND NARRATIVES

Postmodernists have debated the demise of "grand narratives, the challenge to universally agreed stories such as religion or science" (Skinner, 1991). Clark (2006) quotes Peter to define the modern stance as viewing "truth as a product of agreement between rational minds" (p. 394). Postmodernism is defined by Clark as the antithesis of this position:

> Instead, all we have are language games set on a canvas which contains no grounds for adjudicating between the competing claims, nor any epistemic principles for arriving at a unity of knowledge. (p. 394)

Nowhere is the use of metaphorical language more apparent than as "political spectacle," the symbolic language to which we referred in opening the book in Chapter 1 (Smith, Miller-Kahn, Heinecke, & Jarvis, 2004).

One might see this, therefore, as reflecting a postmodernist stance searching for alternative perspectives and manipulation of meaning to gain or to sustain power. However, we would argue that the prevalence of certain metaphors in education talk, though reflecting different provenance and encouraging, in many cases, fuzziness of thought, simultaneously promote a kind of universal belief system. The examples described above of climbing and racing are part of an international trend to promote the feasibility of perfection, or what Pattison (1997) has called mystical management. The latter has a number of facets. First, there is the notion that all children can succeed, and that if effort and practice are appropriate, the failure of some children to achieve can be eradicated. The distribution curve of achievement, the negative impact of persisting poverty on educational performance, the cyclical nature of disadvantage among families are all made invisible. Rather, as the chapters exploring the applicability of the metaphors of machine and accountancy have suggested, educational administrators are part of a global delusion that machine-like consistency and equality of experience are possible. There may no longer be universal belief in an anthropomorphic God or even in the power of rational science but, instead, we have an international dependence on the transforming power of education as a faith of a religious mode. Pattison (1997) notes, "The overtly religious nature of management reaches its apotheosis in some of the language that is used. Here evangelical revivalism appears to have unbridled sway" (p. 39). The latter is invested in the "quality" systems, inspection regimes and million-bit data collection that mechanize our schools, colleges, and universities. "The process of determining organizational direction and structure is governed by visions, mission statements and doom scenarios," says Pattison (1997, p. 39). Education can, of course, transform individual lives and may also make a profound difference to economies at local, regional, and national levels. However, belief that it can be improved to the extent that absolute equality is feasible, reversing millennia of social stratification by means of education, is metaphorically embedded in much contemporary educational discourse and hopelessly delusional. It is, as Pattison (1997) writes, "a world in which beliefs and hopes are more important than facts or empirical realities" (p. 33).

A second universal narrative supported through metaphors is that of the combative educator. This person has warrior-like attributes, translated from the battlefield to the educational context. The adoption of "business-like" attitudes and practice, the determined attempt to maintain or improve a position in comparison with others, the calculation of return on investment, the willingness to crush others to achieve the desired ends have become part of a persona that is admired (Jeffrey, 2002).

Such a persona is universally feted in business (O'Boyle, 1998), but only since the 1990s onwards have such behaviors drawn a positive response when connected to educators. This is not, of course, to suggest that all school leaders behave in this way or share a universal system of such values. However, the line of argument and the evidence presented in the chapters on the leader as lunatic, accountant, and warrior are sufficient to uphold our thesis here, that a kind of hard, ruthless, and so-called "bottom line" administrator is hired and retained because such qualities are admired and, more than admired, seen as necessary by governing boards and funding agencies as a form of social survival in a mercilessly Darwinistic, "dog eat dog" competitive economic fight to the finish. (Perryman, 2006). The political doom scenarios that set the stage for the establishment of these portraits of the necessary educational leader rest on what Fischer (1970) has called "the fallacy of the possible proof" (p. 53). In this instance, a claim, or a metaphor, is not considered true or false by the facts, but rather by "establishing the possibility of its truth or falsity" (p. 53). This approach is utilized when a claim implicit in a metaphor is not itself demonstrable. The parallelism in education is that, if enough people claim the schools are failing, it must be so. One cannot think about the schools without also thinking, "they need to be fixed" (see Emery & Ohanian, 2004, p. 6).

Such intentions are rarely made public and explicit. Nobody has recruited a school principal or superintendent or university president by requiring a competence in treating staff ruthlessly. Nevertheless, the language hints at what is sought. In October 2009, an advertisement for a university president in the UK described the qualities required as including "a track-record of innovation, commercial acumen and demonstrable commitment to the delivery of services that are aligned with the University's vision and purpose" (THES Jobs, 2009, n.p.n.). The purpose is to maintain a top-ranking position. A second advertisement from the same source on the same date suggested that a president's "general management and leadership skills will most likely have been developed within an international context in a university or business." The sister site for jobs for school principals advertised for a principal who can "lead the Academy community to improve further and faster" (TES Connect, 2009). The salary is described tellingly as "competitive." As discussed in Chapter 4, metaphors promote a specific worldview. Hartmann-Mahmud (2002) distinguishes the use of sacred and profane language. Most publicly used educational discourse uses sacred language: empowering, nurturing, inclusive, and collegial. Our exploration of metaphors in earlier chapters has exposed the profane behavior exhibited in many instances: dehumanized, detached, autocratic, and competitively cutthroat. Just as metaphors stimulate awareness of similarity and dissimilarity, the narrative of the new educational leader, combative and focused on test-score improvements and cost-reduction tactics, is easily recognizable but not necessarily noted.

The metaphorical exploration that we have undertaken alerts us to the growth of a universal prototype of the effective leader, whose values differ considerably from the *primus inter pares,* first among equals, head teacher of the first half of the twentieth century. The growing belief that acumen, and specifically business acumen, determination, and drive toward improvement goals are what are needed reflects a value change (Emery & Ohanion, 2004). The metaphors from sports, war, accountancy, and machines that litter educational discourse subtly embed a particular vision of educational administrators or, as Harold Levy remarked, the need is for school administrators to exercise "ruthless leadership" (as quoted in Eisinger & Hula, 2008, p. 115). Goatly (2002) argues that "metaphors . . . partly constitute what it is possible to say about education at a particular historical moment and therefore what education can be" (p. 265). He suggests that ideological wars are played out by one set of metaphors replacing another, and so becoming accepted as natural. In effect, they become dead metaphors as we no longer think about their implications.

Eliot's (1944/1970) lines of verse are relevant here: "Human kind cannot bear very much reality" (p. 14). The open promotion of a managerial, dehumanized approach to educational administration would not be acceptable to many (Samier & Lumby, 2010). The undisguised reality would not be acceptable. It is in the language, and particularly in the metaphors, that the new educational order is insinuated, enshrined, and extended.

POSITIVE METAPHORS

What words we use to speak or write of administrators and students, then, matters much. As Henze and Arriaza (2006) proffer:

> Any serious effort to reform schools to be more equitable and socially just . . . has to consider the role of language in constructing the social identities of those who make up the school community and the power relations among them. . . . Discourse not only mirrors their practice, it is their practice. (p. 164)

We began this chapter by suggesting that metaphors potentially have the power to inspire in a positive way. What, then, is the language that will support a dual aim? First, to support educational leaders, that they may be enabled to conduct their professional lives in a way that is humane; that is not alienated from compassion and connectedness to others. Second, that they should lead it in a way that moves the school and wider community toward greater social justice. The latter is not a grand dream of perfect equality and universal success, but a more modest determination to make a contribution to eradicate some injustice.

First, we ought to differentiate between "caring" and "compassion." While one finds the concept of "caring" in the literature of educational administration (Beck, 1994), it is within what exists in terms of linking schools to student outcomes and "rethinking organizational structures" (Beck, 1994, p. 58). It is possible to "care" about injustice without taking any action to confront or change it (English, 2008a, pp. 5–6). On the other hand, "compassion" is much more radical, because it is the lever for action or *ahimsa*, a metaphor in the mind of one of the greatest agents for social change in the human experience, Mohandas Gandhi, who defined it as "a refusal to submit to injustice" (Iyer, 1973, p. 183).

Murphy (2002) suggests the metaphor of a steward. This metaphor is often used in relation to environmental issues (Brown & Mitchell, 2000). Stewards are those who carefully husband natural resources, believing that they must be protected for future generations. Stewardship does not figure much in talk about educational administrators. The metaphor, however, may be powerful in what it suggests about possibilities. It communicates a primary notion of resisting destruction. Our chapters have used metaphors to explore just how much seems to have been destroyed in our schools and how much more is in danger. For example, Chapter 8 on leaders as lunatics charted the destruction of human relationships between leaders and faculty as well as leaders and children. Chapter 5, using sports as a metaphor, depicted a kind of masculinization of administration and a fiercely competitive rather than nurturing stance. By contrast, above all a steward stands in humility, recognizing that the obligation is to care for that which has worth at least as great as her or himself, and reflects a continuity stretching back and forwards in time. When applied to environmental issues, a steward recognizes the intrinsic worth of all life forms and the moral imperative to preserve each and every one. Similarly, a school steward recognizes the value of every student and the right of that child or young person to be seen as worthy of care and support as any other. Such a stance is a long way from viewing all students as potential achievers of grades, contributors to test scores, or fodder to feed the economy. We are not suggesting that passing tests does not matter. Rather, we suggest that a steward would see this achievement as a part of a holistic picture of an individual's worth, and not as the primary value. A second level of meaning is suggested by Murphy (2002), who uses the term "moral steward." What is to be protected and preserved goes beyond individual students and relates to the values that must be communicated to each generation as it experiences education. We can have no accurate idea of the long-term impact on society or on schools, where faculty and students inhabit a world driven by bureaupathology, when alienation and anomie prevail, and the environment, driven by performative pressures, is not so much immoral as amoral (Samier & Lumby, 2010). However, it does not seem likely that the impact on our society will be good, and we might, in caution, act to prevent potential damage.

A second metaphor that may have some use in communicating what a school leader might be is that of teacher. It relates to the title, still widely used in the UK, of the leader of a school as head teacher. One might see a head teacher as a literal rather than a metaphoric role. Some principals, especially in small elementary or primary schools, do teach class. However, as administrator, the role is increasingly separated from teaching and many principals do not teach at all. Applied to the administrator, the term "teacher" has resonance through history with the great teachers; Jesus, Mohammed, Buddha, and the Zen Masters, all of whom used stories and metaphors to communicate values. This is not a sacrilegious comparison; rather, it suggests that the role of the administrator carries something of the moral burden of those great teachers, and the potential to profoundly influence those with whom they come into contact. It is in part through language that this is achieved. The reference to sacred language earlier in this chapter reported Hartmann-Mahmud's (2002) view that language was used to obscure the underlying real and profane values. Sacred language could, however, be differently understood: Language could be used not to obscure, not to defend the indefensible, but to inspire, to strengthen and to direct to core values. The school leader as teacher implies a reversion to education as a means of developing the whole person, spiritually, aesthetically, intellectually, and physically. It implies the humanist values embedded in mid-twentieth-century attitudes, embedded, for example, in the Plowden Report on primary education in the UK (Central Advisory Council for Education, 1967). The report's description of the aims of education has not been bettered:

> Children need to be themselves, to live with other children and with grown ups, to learn from their environment, to enjoy the present, to get ready for the future, to create and to love, to learn to face adversity, to behave responsibly: in a word, to be human beings. (para. 507)

The leader as teacher encompasses all this. The implied values relate to faculty, as much as to students. The work of Sen (1984) and Nussbaum (1999) has contributed to the United Nations' index of quality of life: "An important starting point is human dignity, the dignity of individuals to live a life they value" (Gagnon & Cornelius, 2000, p. 71). Assessment of any measure designed to achieve equality or justice is directed to take account not just of output measures, but of the impact of process. The goal of the leader as steward or as teacher is to enable students and faculty to live a life they value in the present and in the future. Education is not merely a means of achieving accreditation as a currency for exchange. Future success paid for with current misery, and for many students school is misery, and is no bargain.

SO, WHERE TO NOW?

CONTEXT

Our exploration of metaphors of and for leadership has suggested that the context in which school leaders work in the early twenty-first century comprises unremitting and compelling pressures that potentially distort and destroy human relations and diminish a set of goals for education that predates the accountability movement with all of its efficiency indices and metrics for saleable skills in a market-driven economy centered on for-profit models. Our schools are in danger of becoming primarily a reductive vehicle for competition between individuals and between nations. It is a situation summarized aptly by Pierre Bourdieu (1998) in his book *Acts of Resistance: Against the Tyranny of the Market*, who warned that we have confused "things of logic for the logic of things" (p. 101). That the current emphasis on standardization and rationality comprising greater efficiency within a machine bureaucracy is not working for nations as a whole is proffered by the fact that the United States and Britain are the second and third countries in the world where income inequality is the greatest ("The rich, the poor and the growing gap," 2006). In the US, "the typical American chief executive now earns 300 times the average wage, up tenfold from the 1970s" (p. 30). The current approach to educational reform as we have argued is not likely to change such inequalities anytime soon. In fact, such inequalities are more than likely to be continued and reinforced.

Many school administrators and faculty are profoundly committed to the well-being of children. Their distress at the influences brought to bear that compromise their values that prioritize the well-being of children is evident in much research (Ball, 2003; Blackmore, 2004; Brooks; Emery & Ohanian; Jeffrey, 2002; Wilson & Hall, 2002). The destructive effect on children is also documented (Johnson, Johnson, Farenga, & Ness, 2008; Locker & Cropley, 2004; Saltman, 2000). Many researchers have analyzed the impact of the context, variously described as new public management (Deem, 1998; Hood, 1995; Pattison, 1997), managerialism (Simkins, 2000) or performativity (Butler, 1997).

In this book we have proffered what we hope is a further perspective. Through metaphors we have attempted to challenge administrators to confront what they know is not so, but also is so. Leaders are not lunatics or warriors or sports coaches; it is not so. Yet, in some sense, the nature of each of these roles has become embedded in school leadership; it is so. Our challenge is both intellectual and emotional; that leaders recognize what they may have become or are in danger of becoming, and judge whether this is as they wish or not, and act.

LEADERSHIP PRACTICE

The Plowden Report (Central Advisory Council for Education, 1967) rather acerbically reminded readers that "general statements of aims were of limited value, and that a pragmatic approach to the purposes of education was more likely to be fruitful" (para. 501). Intending to develop children as human beings is one thing; what this means leaders must do is another. Many might argue that there is limited room for maneuver. National and state mandates shape practice, yet some room for maneuver remains. Shain and Gleeson (1999) noted that staff members react to imposed policies with resistance, willing acceptance, and, a third category, "strategic compliance" (p. 456). The last stance accepts some aspects of policy, rejects others, bends rules, and filters action though values. Some of the most destructive behaviors explored in this book reflect acceptance, willing or otherwise, of the pressure of inspection, for example, or of insensitive attitudes to faculty, or of competitive behaviors toward other organizations. Many other administrators maintain a compassionate and humane stance in making choices about how to lead and to act. However, as the evidence presented in earlier chapters suggests, many may succumb to the pressures of the context and behave in dysfunctional or amoral ways. Strategic compliers adopt a middle way. They do not reject outright all change demanded by policy; rather, they filter possibilities through their value system and act with shrewdness to accommodate to some degree, and to deflect or adapt, as their values dictate. Their primary contribution to the education of students is the model they present of values-based behavior.

The possibility of retaining humanity and achieving the goal of living a life that is valued is not entirely under administrators' control. Weber (1958/2003) argued not only that increasingly rational and efficient forms of bureaucracy would create social dislocation, but that individuals would lose the ability to imagine anything different. They are so trapped in Weber's "iron cage" (p. 181) of rational structures and laws, so habituated to confinement, that the possibility of an alternative way of being becomes ever more remote and unreal. A major responsibility for shaping leadership behaviors lies, therefore, with the policy makers who continue to impose demands for ever more intensified, competitive, and mechanized leadership. Though strategic compliance will lend leaders some freedom, it is a partial and unsatisfactory response for, as Bottery (2004) reminds us:

> The nation-state [that] finds itself in competition with other nation-states for the citizen-consumer's business, and rather than being a body concerned with a "public good"—a concern for all—. . . becomes increasingly concerned with selling its "services" to the highest bidder, and in the process its activity, its very language, is captured by the market. (p. 75)

The primary responsibility for the parlous state of education, insofar as people have influence, lies with the policy makers that have racked our schools with reductive and dehumanizing processes, following the metaphors of market efficiency, and leadership models based on accounting and the characteristics of machine bureaucracy (Mintzberg, 1983). Until these are lifted and replaced with processes more humane for the schools, it is unreasonable and unrealistic to imagine that educational leaders can meet the needs of future citizens other than by limiting, through strategic compliance and resistance, the degree of dysfunction in the schools caused by misapplied policy metaphors.

LEADERSHIP DEVELOPMENT NEEDS

Competence and standards-based training will neither equip leaders to engineer strategic compliance, nor develop confidence in their value base. The development of school administrators, of course, will need to ensure that there is a sound basis of understanding of the process of learning. Brooks (2006) has recommended that the first thing that school reformers should provide teachers with in advocating change is an answer to the question, "How does participating in this activity make the school more conducive to student learning? And, by extension, how does participating in this reform activity make me a better teacher?" (p. 176). The answer should not be one where children are homogenized on one-dimensional scales of development (mathematics, science, and technology), but fully differentiated on all of the dimensions that a fully functioning, confident, compassionate future citizen of the world is nurtured.

Beyond that, leaders will need to have a critical perspective on the wider context and the forces at play that support or impede learning. They will need support to develop and articulate their value base and to understand its provenance in their own history and identity. They will need to be sensitized to their own and others' use of language and its significance for learning. Though practice-based apprenticeship will always have a place, the substitution of philosophy, literature, drama, and sociology for standards-based checklist assessment would provide a more appropriate preparation than the narrow scientism and behaviorism that dominate graduate programs and curricula in too many universities today (see English & Papa, 2010). Instead of producing factory foremen, driving workers toward improved profits, they could be aiming to produce the stewards and head teachers that our children deserve, and our society needs.

References

Abramowitz, J. S., Whiteside, S. P., & Deacon, B. J. (2005). The effectiveness of treatment for pediatric obsessive-compulsive disorder: A meta-analysis. *Behavior Therapy, 36*, 55–63. Retrieved January 28, 2009, from http://www.mayoclinic.org/news2005-av/AbramowitzOCD.pdf.

Adelman, C. (2006, October 13). The propaganda of numbers. *The Chronicle of Higher Education, 53*(8), pp. B6—B9.

Albergotti, R. (2009, April 24). Snap judgments in the NFL. *The Wall Street Journal*, p. W5.

Alexander, B. K., Anderson, G. L., & Gallegos, B. P. (2005). *Performance theories in education: Power, pedagogy, and the politics of identity.* London: Lawrence Erlbaum.

Anderson, A. (2005). Enacted metaphor: The theatricality of the entrepreneurial process. *International Small Business Journal, 23*(6), 587–603.

Anderson, J. L. (1997). *Che Guevara: A revolutionary life.* New York: Grove Press.

Araújo, M. (2005). Disrup*tive* or disrup*ted*? A qualitative study on the construction of indiscipline. *International Journal of Inclusive Education, 9*(3), 241–268.

Archer, T., & Fletcher-Campbell, F. (2005). *Admissions/place planning probe.* Slough, UK: National Foundation for Educational Research.

Armstrong, K. (1992). *Muhammad: A biography of the prophet.* San Francisco: HarperCollins.

Armstrong, K. (1993). *A history of God.* New York: Ballantine Books.

Armstrong, K. (2005). *A short history of myth.* Edinburgh, UK: Canongate.

Aun, T. K., Riley, J. P. II, Atputhasamy, L., & Subramaniam, R. (2006). School science achievement in Japan and Singapore: A tale of two cities. *Educational Research for Policy and Practice, 5*, 1–13.

Bailey, F. G. (1977). *Morality and expediency.* Oxford, UK: Blackwell.

Bakan, J. (2004). *The corporation: The pathological pursuit of profit and power.* New York: Free Press.

Baker, M. (2007, September 25). How to ride out a media storm. *Guardian*, p. 6. Retrieved April 1, 2010, from http://browse.guardian.co.uk/search/all/Education?lDim=N%3D3093&search=how+to+ride+out+a+media+storm&year=2007&search_target=%2Fsearch&fr=cb-guardian.

Ball, S. (1997). Good school/bad school: Paradox and fabrication. *British Journal of the Sociology of Education, 18*(3), 317–336.

Ball, S. (2003). The teacher's soul and the terrors of performativity. *Journal of Education Policy, 18*(2), 215–228.

Banks, R. (2000). Moving from faith to faithfulness. In R. Banks & K. Powell (Eds.), *Faith in leadership: How leaders live out their faith in their work—and why it matters* (pp. 3–18). San Francisco: Jossey-Bass.

Barber, M. (1991). Educational daftness: Teachers' objections to SATS—and the alternatives. *Education, 177*(20), 400.

Barnhart, R. (1995). *The Barnhart concise dictionary of etymology.* New York: HarperCollins.

Bass, B. M., & Avolio, B. J. (1990). *Transformational leadership development: Manual for the multifactor leadership questionnaire.* Binghamton, NY: Center for Leadership Studies, State University of New York.

Bauman, Z. (2004). *Identity.* Cambridge, UK: Polity Press.

Beck, L. (1994). *Reclaiming educational administration as a caring profession.* New York: Teachers College Press.

Beck, L. G., & Murphy, J. (1993). *Understanding the principalship: Metaphorical themes 1920s–1990s.* New York: Teachers College Press.

Beckett, C. (2003). The language of siege: Military metaphors in the spoken language of social work. *British Journal of Social Work, 33*(5), 625–639.

Beecher, T. (1989). Principles and politics: An interpretive framework for university management. In A. Westoby (Ed.), *Culture and power in educational organizations* (pp. 317–327). Milton Keynes, UK: Open University Press.

Begley, P. (2003). In pursuit of authentic school leadership practices. In P. Begley & O. Johansson (Eds.), *The ethical dimensions of school leadership.* London: Kluwer Academic.

Bell, T. (1988). *The thirteenth man: A Reagan cabinet memoir.* New York: The Free Press.

Bentham, J. (1787). *Panopticon: Or, the inspection-house.* Dublin: Thomas Byrne.

Bergman, I. (1990). *Images: My life in film.* (M. Ruth, Trans.). New York: Arcade.

Bersin, A. (2005, April 20). Making schools productive: The point of accountability and the key to renewal. *Education Week, 24*(32), 40.

Bharwani, V. (2006, September 26). Does new banding system really ease pressure on kids—or make it worse? *The New Paper.*

Bidwell, C. (1965). The school as a formal organization. In J. G. March (Ed.), *Handbook of organizations* (pp. 972–1022). Chicago: Rand McNally.

Bjork, L. (2000). Introduction: Women in the superintendency—Advances in research and theory. *Educational Administration Quarterly, 36*(1), 5–17.

Black, R. A. (2006). What did Adam Smith say about self-love? *Journal of Markets and Morality, 9*(1), 7–34.

Blackmore, J. (2004). Leading as emotional management work in high risk times: The counterintuitive impulses of performativity and passion. *School Leadership & Management, 24*(4), 439–459.

Blair, T. (2005, October 5). *Speech on education at 10 Downing Street.* Retrieved December 30, 2009, from http://www.number10.gov.uk/Page8363.

Boje, D. M. (1996). *Management education as a panoptic cage—Rethinking management education.* London: Sage.

Bolton, C., & English, F. (2009). My head and my heart: De-constructing the historical/hysterical binary that conceals and reveals emotion in educational leadership. In E. Samier & M. Schmidt (Eds.), *Emotional dimensions of educational administration and leadership* (pp. 125–142). Abingdon, UK: Routledge.

Bono, J. E., Foldes, H. J., Vinson, G., & Muros, J. P. (2007). Workplace emotions: The role of supervision and leadership. *Journal of Applied* Psychology, *92*(5), 1357–1367.

Boorstin, D. (1987). *The image: A guide to pseudo-events in America.* Chicago: University of Chicago Press.

Booth, W. C. (1979). Metaphor as rhetoric: The problem of evaluation. In S. Sacks (Ed.), *On metaphor* (pp. 44– 70). Chicago: University of Chicago Press.

Bottery, M. (2004). *The challenges of educational leadership.* London: Paul Chapman.

Bourdieu, P. (1984). *Distinction: A social critique of the judgment of taste.* (R. Nice, Trans.). Cambridge, MA: Harvard University Press.

Bourdieu, P. (1998). *Acts of resistance: Against the tyranny of the market.* (R. Nice, Trans.). New York: The New Press.

Bourdieu, P. (2001). *Firing back: Against the tyranny of the market, 2* (L. Waquant, Trans.). New York: The New Press.

Bowdle, B. F. (2005). The career of metaphor. *Psychological Review, 12*(1), 193–216.

Bowe, R., Ball, S., & Gewirtz, S. (1994). 'Parental choice,' consumption and social theory: The operation of micro-markets in education. *British Journal of Educational Studies, 42*(1), 38–52.

Boyle, D. (2001, January 14). You can count me out. *The Observer Review*, p. 1.

Bozeman, B., & Rainey, H. G. (1998). Organizational rules and the "bureaucratic personality." *American Journal of Political Science, 42*(1), 165–189.

Brecht, B. (1964). *Brecht on theatre: The development of an aesthetic* (J. Willett, Ed. & Trans.). London: Methuen.

Brehony, K. J., & Deem, R. (2005). Challenging the post-Fordist/flexible organisation thesis: The case of reformed educational organisations. *British Journal of Sociology of Education, 26*(3), 395–414.

The Broad Foundation & Thomas B. Fordham Institute. (2003). Better Leaders for America's Schools: A Manifesto. In Y. Lasley, II (Ed.), *Better Leaders for America's Schools: Perspectives on the Manifesto* (pp. 12-35). Columbia, MO: University Council for Educational Administration.

Broadfoot, P. (1991). *Looking back in anger?: Findings from the PACE project concerning primary teachers' experiences of SATs. Primary assessment, curriculum and experience.* Unpublished manuscript.

Brock, D. (2005). *The Republican noise machine: Right-wing media and how it corrupts democracy.* New York: Three Rivers Press.

Brooks, J. (2006). *The dark side of school reform.* Lanham, MD: Rowman & Littlefield Education.

Brown, F. (1995). *Zola: A life.* New York: Farrar, Straus & Giroux.

Brown, J., & Mitchell, B. (2000). Landscape stewardship: New directions in conservation of nature and culture. *The George Wright Forum, 17*(1), 70–79. Retrieved May 22, 2006, from www.georgewright.org/171brown.pdf.

Brush, S. (2006, October 30). A vote of no confidence. *US News and World Report*, p. 56.

Burns, E. (1972). *Theatricality: A study of convention in the theatre and in social life.* Harlow, UK: Longman.

Burns, J. M. (1978). *Leadership.* New York: Harper & Row.

Bush, T., Coleman, M., & Glover, D. (1993). *Managing autonomous schools: The grant-maintained experience.* London: Paul Chapman.

Bussert-Webb, K. (n.d.). *The teacher's testing panopticon*. Retrieved August 7, 2009, from http://www.und.nodak.edu/dept/ehd/journal/Summer%202004/bussert.html.

Butler, J. (1997). *Excitable speech: A politics of the performative*. London: Routledge.

Caiden, G. E. (1991). What really is public maladministration? *Public Administration Review, 51*(6), 486–493.

Callahan, D. (2004). *The cheating culture: Why more Americans are doing wrong to get ahead*. Orlando, FL: Harcourt.

Cameron, D. (2009, October 8). *Putting Britain back on her feet*. Speech given to Conservative Party conference. Retrieved April 5, 2010, from http://www.conservatives.com/News/Speeches/2009/10/David_Cameron_Putting_Britain_back_on_her_feet.aspx.

Camp, E. (2005). Josef Stern, metaphor in context. *Noûs, 39*(4), 715–731.

Campbell, J., & Moyers, B. (1991). *The power of myth*. New York: Anchor Books.

Canguilheim, G. (1988). *Ideology and rationality in the history of the life sciences*. Cambridge: MIT Press.

Carter, C., & Osler, A. (2000). Human rights, identities and conflict management: A study of school culture as experienced thorough classroom relationships. *Cambridge Journal of Education, 30*(3), 335–356.

Cassuto, L. (2009, April 21). John Madden made us smarter. *The Wall Street Journal*, p. D9.

Central Advisory Council for Education. (1967). *Children and their primary schools: A report of the Central Advisory Council for Education: The report* (Vol. 1). London: Her Majesty's Stationery Office. Retrieved March 29, 2010, from http://www.educationengland.org.uk/documents/plowden/plowden1-00.html.

Chandler, D. G. (1987). *The military maxims of Napoleon*. New York: Macmillan.

Chernow, R. (1998). *Titan: The life of John D. Rockefeller, Sr*. New York: Vintage.

Cherryholmes, C. (1988). *Power and criticism: Post-structural investigations in education*. New York: Teachers College Press.

Clark, J. A. (2006). Michael Peters' Lyotardian account of postmodernism and education: Some epistemic problems and naturalistic solutions. *Educational Philosophy and Theory, 38*(3), 391–405.

Cleary, T. (1991). *The Japanese art of war*. London: Shambala.

Clegg, S. (2001). Theorising the machine: Gender, education and computing. *Gender and Education, 13*(3), 307–324.

Clough, D. (1984). *Decisions in public and private sectors: Theories, practices, and processes*. Englewood Cliffs, NJ: Prentice Hall.

Coates, G., & Adnett, N. (2002, September). *Encouraging cream-skimming and dreg-siphoning? Increasing competition between English HEIs*. Paper presented at the European Conference on Educational Research, University of Lisbon, Portugal. Retrieved January 26, 2009, from http://www.leeds.ac.uk/educol/documents/00002369.htm.

Cohen, T. (1979). Metaphor and the cultivation of intimacy. In S. Sacks (Ed.), *On metaphor* (pp.1–10). Chicago: University of Chicago Press.

Collins, A., Ireson, J., Stubbs, S., Nash, K., & Burnside, P. (2006). *New models of headship: Federations: Does every primary school need a headteacher? Key implications from a study of federations in The Netherlands*. Nottingham, UK: NCSL.

Collins, J. (2001). *Good to great*. New York: HarperCollins.

Collinson, D. (2003). Identities and insecurities: Selves at work. *Organization, 10*(3), 527–547.

Conger, J. (1989). *The charismatic leader: Behind the mystique of exceptional leadership.* San Francisco: Jossey-Bass.

Connor, M. J. (2003). Pupil stress and standard assessment tasks (SATS): An update. *Emotional and Behavioural Difficulties, 8*(2), 101–107.

Cornelissen, J. P. (2002). On the "organizational identity" metaphor. *British Journal of Management, 13,* 259–268.

Cornelissen, J. P. (2004). What are we playing at? Theatre, organization, and the use of metaphor. *Organization Studies, 25*(5), 705–726.

Cousins, N. (1987). *The pathology of power.* New York: W.W. Norton & Company.

Covey, S. (1990). *The seven habits of highly effective people.* New York: Simon & Schuster.

Crosby, P. (1984). *Quality without tears.* New York: McGraw-Hill.

Crossant, J. (1994). *Jesus: A revolutionary biography.* San Francisco: HarperCollins.

Cuban, L. (2004). *The blackboard and the bottom line.* Cambridge, MA: Harvard University Press.

D'Este, C. (1995). *Patton: A genius for war.* New York: HarperCollins.

Deely, M. (Producer), & Scott, R. (Director). (1982). *Blade Runner* [Motion Picture]. United States: The Ladd Company.

Deem, R. (1998). "New managerialism" and higher education: The management of performances and cultures in universities in the United Kingdom. *International Studies in Sociology of Education, 8*(1), 47–70.

Demack, S., Drew, D., & Grimsley, M. (2000). Minding the gap: Ethnic, gender and social class differences in attainment at 16, 1988–95. *Race Ethnicity and Education, 3*(2), 117–143.

Deming, W. E. (1982). *Quality, productivity and competitive position.* Cambridge: MIT Press.

Deming, W. E. (1986). *Out of the crisis.* Cambridge: MIT Press.

Department for Children, Schools and Families. (2004). *Children's Act 2004.* London: The Stationery Office.

Department for Children, Schools and Families. (2009a). Children's Act summary. Retrieved August 13, 2009, from http://www.childrens-commissioner.co.uk/html/aboutus3.html.

Department for Children, Schools and Families. (2009b). *Departmental Report 2009.* Norwich, UK: The Stationery Office.

Department for Education and Skills, & Ofsted (2006). *Improving performance through school self-evaluation and improvement planning.* London: HMSO. Retrieved August 14, 2009, from www.ofsted.gov.uk.

Department for Education and Skills. (2004). *National standards for headteachers,* Nottingham, UK: DfES.

Department of Education and Skills. (1991). *Education and training for the 21st century.* London: HMSO.

Dewey, J. (1966). *Democracy and education: An introduction to the philosophy of education.* New York: Free Press. (Original work published 1916)

Dickens, C. (1990). *Hard times.* London: Norton. (Original work published 1854)

Dunham, B. (1964). *Heroes and heretics: A social history of dissent.* New York: Alfred A. Knopf.

Earley, P. (Ed.). (1998). *School improvement after inspection? School and LEA responses.* London: Paul Chapman.

Edward, K. L., & Munro, I. (2008). Depression and other mental illnesses in the context of workplace efficacy. *Journal of Psychiatric and Mental Health Nursing, 15*, 605–611.

Eisinger, P., & Hula, R. (2004). Gunslinger school administrators: Non-traditional leadership in urban school systems in the United States. *Urban Education, 39*(6), 621–637.

Eisinger, P., & Hula, R. (2008). Gunslinger school administrators: Nontraditional leadership in urban school systems in the United States. *Educational leadership* (pp. 111–123). Boston, MA: McGraw-Hill.

Eliot, T. S. (1970). *Four quartets.* London: Faber. (Original work published 1944)

Elliott, G., & Crossley, M. (1997). Contested values in further education: Findings from a case study of the management of change. *Educational Management and Administration, 25*(1), 79–92.

Emery, K., & Ohanian, S. (2004). *Why is corporate America bashing our public schools?* Portsmouth, NH: Heinemann.

English, F. (1994). *Theory in educational administration.* New York: HarperCollins.

English, F. (2004). Learning "manifestospeak": A metadiscursive analysis of the Fordham Institute's and Broad Foundation's manifesto for better leaders for America's schools. In T. J. Lasley (Ed.), *Better leaders for America's schools: Perspectives on the manifesto* (pp. 52–91). Columbia, MO: University Council for Educational Administration.

English, F. (2008a). *Anatomy of professional practice: Promising research perspectives on educational leadership.* Lanham, MD: Rowman & Littlefield Education.

English, F. (2008b). *The art of educational leadership: Balancing performance and accountability.* Thousand Oaks, CA: Sage.

English, F., & Papa, R. (2010). *Restoring human agency to educational administration: Status and strategies.* Lancaster, PA: Pro-Active.

Essig, L., & Owens, L. (2009, October 9). What if marriage is bad for us? *The Chronicle Review,* pp. B4–5.

Failing our children. (2008, November 24). *The Wall Street Journal,* p. R9.

Farnham, D., & Horton, S. (Eds.). (1993). *Managing the new public services.* Basingstoke, UK: Macmillan.

Fields, G. (2008, November 11). DC schools chief scores gains, ruffles feathers. *The Wall Street Journal,* p. A6. Retrieved March 27, 2010, from http://online.wsj.com/article/SB122636956488016241.html.

Fischer, D. (1970). *Historians' fallacies: Toward a logic of historical thought.* New York: Harper Torch.

Flynn, N. (1993). *Public sector management.* London: Harvester & Wheatsheaf.

Forrester, G. (2005). All in a day's work: Primary teachers "performing" and "caring." *Gender and Education, 17*(3), 271–287.

Forsyth, P. B., & Hoy, W. K. (1978). Isolation and alienation in educational organizations. *Educational Administration Quarterly, 14*, 80–96.

Foucault, M. (1977). *Discipline and punish: The birth of the prison* (A. Sheridan, Trans.). New York: Vintage Books.

Fowler, H. W., & Fowler, F. G. (Eds.). (1964). *The concise Oxford dictionary* (5th ed.). Oxford, UK: Oxford University Press.

Fox, L. (2003). *Enron: The rise and fall.* New York: John Wiley & Sons.

Frank, R., & Efrati, A. (2009, June 30). "Evil" Madoff gets 150 years in epic fraud. *The Wall Street Journal,* p. A1.

Fraser, D. (1993). *Knight's cross: A life of Field Marshall Erwin Rommel.* New York: HarperCollins.

Freidman, C. P. (2000). The marvellous medical education machine, *or* how medical education can be 'unstuck' in time. *Medical Teacher, 22*(5), 496–502.

Freire, P. (1996). *Pedagogy of the oppressed* (M. Bergman Ramos, Trans.). London: Penguin Education. (Original work published 1972)

Frick, D. (2004). *Robert K. Greenleaf: A life of servant leadership.* San Francisco: Berrett-Koehler Publishers.

Frymer-Kensky, T. (1996). Women. In P. Achtemeier (Ed.), *Bible dictionary* (pp. 1218–1220). San Francisco: HarperCollins.

Fullan, M. (2009). Leadership development: The larger context. *Educational Leadership, 67*(2), 45–49.

Funk, R., Hoover, R., & The Jesus Seminar. (1993). *The five gospels: The search for the authentic words of Jesus.* New York: Macmillan Publishing.

Gabler, N. (1998). *Life: The movie.* New York: Vintage Books Division of Random House.

Gagnon, S., & Cornelius, N. (2000). Re-examining workplace equality: The capabilities approach. *Human Resource Management Journal, 10*(4), 68–87.

Galbraith J. K. (1983). *On the anatomy of power.* Boston: Houghton Mifflin.

Gardner, H. (1995). *Leading minds: The anatomy of leadership.* New York: Basic Books.

Gawthorp, L. C. (1971). *Administrative politics and social change.* New York: St. Martin's Press.

Geertz, C. (1993). *The interpretation of cultures.* London: Fontana.

Gerstner, L. (2002). *Who says elephants can't dance?* New York: HarperCollins.

Gerstner, L. (2008, December 1). Lessons from 40 years of education "reform." *The Wall Street Journal,* p. A23.

Gewirtz, S., Ball, S. J., & Bowe, E. R. (1995). *Markets, choice and equity in education.* Buckingham, UK: Open University Press.

Gibson, A., & Asthana, S. (2000). Local markets and the polarization of public-sector schools in England and Wales. *Transactions of the Institute of British Geographers, 25*(3), 303–319.

Giddens, A. (1976). *New rules of sociological method.* London: Hutchinson.

Giles, C. (2006). Sustaining secondary school visions over time: Resistance, resilience and educational reform. *Journal of Educational Change, 7*(3), 179–208.

Gillborn, D. (2004). Anti-racism: From policy to praxis. In G. Ladson-Billings & D. Gillborn (Eds.), *The RoutledgeFalmer reader in multicultural education.* Abingdon, UK: RoutledgeFalmer.

Gillborn, D. (2005). Education policy as an act of white supremacy: Whiteness, critical race theory and education reform. *Journal of Education Policy, 20*(4), 485–505.

Giuliani, R. W. (2002). *Leadership.* New York: Hyperion.

Glader, P., & Scannell, K. (2009, August 5). GE settles civil-fraud charges. *The Wall Street Journal,* p. B2.

Glatter, R., & Harvey, J. (2006). *New models of headship. Varieties of shared headship: A preliminary exploration.. A report prepared for the National College for School Leadership.* Nottingham, UK: NCSL.

Goatly, A. (2002). Conflicting metaphors in the Hong Kong special administrative region educational reform proposals. *Metaphor and Symbol, 17*(4), 263–294.

Goffman, E. (1959). *The presentation of self in everyday life.* Middlesex, UK: Penguin.

Goldstein, B., & Rosselli, F. (2003). Etiological paradigms of depression: The relationship between perceived causes, empowerment, treatment preferences, and stigma. *Journal of Mental Health, 12*(6), 551–563.

Goodwin, C. (1996). Moving the drama into the factory: The contribution of metaphors to services research. *European Journal of Marketing, 30*(9), 13–36.

Gorard, S., Lumby, J., Briggs, A., Morrison, M., Hall, I., Maringe, F., et al. (2009). *National report on the 14–19 reform programme: Baseline of evidence 2007–2008.* Birmingham, UK: University of Birmingham.

Gove, M. (2009, October 7). *Failing schools need new leadership.* Speech given to the Conservative Party. Manchester, UK. Retrieved October 19, 2009, from http://www.conservatives.com/News/Speeches/2009/10/Michael_Gove_Failing_schools_need_new_leadership.aspx.

Grace, P. (1984). *Burning money: The waste of your tax dollars.* New York: Macmillan.

Grant, U. S. (1885). *Personal memoirs of U. S. Grant, Vol. 1.* New York: Charles L. Webster & Company.

Greenberg, S. (1999). Previous convictions: "I used to be a perfectionist, but now I realise it is the plague of modern life." *Prospect Magazine.* Retrieved April 5, 2010, from http://www.prospectmagazine.co.uk/1999/06/3922-previous convictions/.

Gronn, P. (2003). Leadership's place in a community of practice. In M. Brundrett, N. Burton, & R. Smith (Eds.), *Leadership in education.* London: Paul Chapman.

Gross, B., Booker, T., & Goldhaber, D. (2009). Boosting student achievement: The effect of comprehensive school reform on student achievement. *Educational Evaluation and Policy Analysis, 32*(2), 111–126.

Grun, B. (1991). *The timetables of history.* New York: Simon & Schuster.

Gudykunst, W. (1995). Anxiety/uncertainty management (AUM) theory. In R. Wiseman (Ed.), *International Communication Theory, Vol. XIX* (pp. 8–58). London: Sage.

Gunter, H. (2004). Remodelling the school workforce: Developing perspectives on headteacher workload. *Management in Education, 18*(3), 6–11.

Gunter, H., & Butt, G. (2005). Challenging modernization: Remodelling the education workforce. *Educational Review, 57*(2), 131–137.

Hage, J. (1965, December). An axiomatic theory of organizations. *Administrative Science Quarterly, 10*(3), 289–320.

Hall, R. H. (1972). *Organizations: Structure and process.* Englewood Cliffs, NJ: Prentice Hall.

Hamilton, G. (2008). Mythos and mental illness: Psychopathy, fantasy, and contemporary moral life [Electronic version]. *Journal of Medical Humanities, 29,* 231–242.

Hanushek, E. (1997). Assessing the results of school resources on student performance: An update. *Educational Evaluation and Policy Analysis, 19,* 141–164.

Harding, J. (2006, October 10). Carly reinvented. *The London Times,* pp. 4–6.

Harnsberger, C. (1964). *Treasury of presidential quotations.* Chicago: Follett Publishing.

Harris, S., Wallace, G., & Ruddock, J. (1995). "It's not that I haven't learned much. It's just that I really don't understand what I'm doing": Metacognition and secondary school students. *Research Papers in Education, 10*(2), 253–271.

Hartley, D. (2007). Education policy and the 'inter'-regnum. *Journal of Education Policy, 22*(6), 695–708.

Hartmann-Mahmud, L. (2002). War as metaphor. *Peace Review, 14*(4), 427–432.

Hasenfeld, Y. (1983). *Human service organizations.* Englewood Cliffs, NJ: Prentice Hall.

Hawkridge, D. (2003). The human in the machine: Reflections on mentoring at the British Open University. *Mentoring & Tutoring: Partnership in Learning, 11*(1), 15–24.

Henze, R., & Arriaza, G. (2006). Language and reforming schools: A case for a critical approach to language in educational leadership. *International Journal of Leadership in Education, 9*(2), 157–177.

Hill, J., & Cheadle, R. (1996). *The Bible tells me so: Uses and abuses of holy scripture.* New York: Anchor Doubleday Books.

HM Treasury. (2006). Leitch review of skills. Prosperity for all in a global economy—world class skills. Final Report. UK.

Hood, C. (1995). The "new public management" in the 1980s: Variations on a theme. *Accounting Organizations and Society, 20*(2/3), 93–109.

Hopmann, S. T. (2008). No child, no school, no state left behind: Schooling in the age of accountability [Electronic version]. *Journal of Curriculum Studies, 40*(4), 417–456.

Horvath, J., Williams, W., Forsythe, G., Sweeney, P., Sternberg, R., McNally, J., et al. (1994). *Tacit knowledge in military leadership: Evidence from officer interviews* (Tech. Rep. No. 1018). Alexandria, VA: United States Army Research Institute for the Behavioral and Social Sciences.

House, E. (1998). *Schools for sale: Why free market policies won't improve America's schools and what will.* New York: Teachers College.

Information for School and College Governors. (2004). *Getting it right: Exclusions.* London: DfES. Retrieved March 18, 2009, from www.teachernet.gov.uk/wholeschool/behaviour/exclusion/gettingitright/.

Ingrassia, P. (2009, March 31). Wagoner had to go. *The Wall Street Journal*, p. A21.

Ishikawa, K. (1985). *What is total quality control? The Japanese way.* London: Prentice Hall.

Iyer, R. (1973). *The moral and political thought of Mahatma Gandhi.* New York: Oxford University Press.

Jacobus, L. (2005). *The Bedford introduction to drama* (5th ed.). Boston: Bedford/St. Martin's.

Jaspers, K. (1963). *General psychopathology.* (J. Hoenig & M. W. Hamilton, Trans.). Manchester, UK: Manchester University Press. (Original work published 1913)

Jeffrey, B. (2002). Performativity and primary teacher relations. *Journal of Educational Policy, 17*(5), 531–546.

Jenkins, R. (2001). *Churchill: A biography.* New York: Farrar, Straus & Giroux.

Johnson, S. (1998). *Who moved my cheese?* New York: G.P. Putnam & Sons.

Johnson, D. D., Johnson, B., Farenga, S. J., & Ness, D. (2008). *Stop high-stakes testing: An appeal to America's conscience.* Lanham, MD: Rowman & Littlefield.

Jones, N. (1999). The changing role of the primary school head: Reflections from the front line. *Educational Management Administration Leadership, 27*(4), 441–451.

Josefowitz, N. (1980). *Paths to power: A woman's guide from first job to top executive.* Reading, MA: Addison-Wesley.

Kaplan, E. (2004). *With God on their side: How Christian fundamentalists trampled science, policy, and democracy in George W. Bush's white house.* New York: The New Press.

Karp, S. (2002). Let them eat tests: Bush bill opens a new era in federal education policy. *Radical Teacher, 65,* 23–26.

Keegan, J. (1982). *Six armies in Normandy: From D-day to the liberation of Paris.* New York: Penguin Books.

Keller, M. (1989). *Rude awakening: The rise, fall, and struggle for recovery of General Motors.* New York: William Morrow.

Kelly, R. (2005, December 16). *Higher standards, better schools for all.* Speech given to LGA conference at Local Government House, London. Retrieved August 13, 2009, from http://www.dcsf.gov.uk/speeches/media/documents/lgahsbs.doc.

Kennedy, H. (1997). *Learning works: Widening participation in further education.* Coventry, UK: FEFC.

Keys, W., Maychell, K., Evans, C., Brooks. R., Lee, B., & Pathak, S. (1998). *Staying on: A study of young people's decisions about school sixth forms, sixth-form colleges and colleges of further education.* Slough: NFER.

Khurana, R. (2002). *Searching for a corporate savior: The irrational quest for charismatic CEOs.* Princeton, NJ: Princeton University Press.

Korac-Kakabadse, A., & Korac-Kakabadse, N. (1997). Best practice in the Australian public service. *Journal of Managerial Psychology, 12*(7), 433–491.

Kornacki, S. (2009, September 2). Why your coach votes Republican. *The Wall Street Journal*, p. B14.

Korten, D. (2001). *When corporations rule the world.* Sterling: Kumarian Press.

Koskela, H. (2000). "The gaze without eyes": Video-surveillance and the changing nature of urban space. *Progress in Human Geography, 24*(2), 243–265.

Kouzes, J. M., & Posner, B. Z. (2002). *The leadership challenge.* San Francisco: Jossey-Bass.

Kroska, A., & Harkness, S. K. (2008). Exploring the role of diagnosis in the modified labeling theory of mental illness. *Social Psychology Quarterly, 71*(2), 193–208.

Kupermintz, H. (2003). Teacher effects and teacher effectiveness: A validity investigation of the Tennessee value added assessment system. *Educational Evaluation and Policy Analysis, 25*, 287–298.

Lakoff, G., & Johnson, M. (2003). *Metaphors we live by* (2nd ed.). Chicago: University of Chicago Press.

Lassman, P., & Spiers, R. (Eds.). (1994). *Weber: Political writings.* Cambridge, UK: Cambridge University Press.

Lawless, C. (1991). *The Civil War sourcebook: A traveler's guide.* New York: Harmony Books.

Lawton, C. & Clark, D. (2007, August 12). Dell to restate 4 years of results. *The Wall Street Journal,* p. A3.

Leithwood, K., & Jantzi, D. (2005a). Transformational school leadership. In Davies, B. (Ed.), *The essentials of school leadership.* London: Paul Chapman.

Leithwood, K., & Jantzi, D. (2005b, April). *A review of transformational school leadership research 1996–2005.* Paper presented at the American Educational Research Association Annual Meeting, Montreal, Quebec, Canada.

Leithwood, K., Day, C., Sammons, P., Harris, A., & Hopkins, D. (2006). *Successful school leadership: What it is and how it influences pupil learning* (DfES Research Report 800). NCSL/DfES. Retrieved March 31, 2010, from http://www.dcsf.gov.uk/rsgateway/DB/RRP/u014998/index.shtml.

Leney, T., Lucas, N., & Taubaum, D. (1998). *Learning funding: The impact of FEFC funding. Evidence from twelve colleges.* London: University of London, Institute of Education & NATFHE.

Lessinger, L., & Gillis, D. (1976). *Teaching as a performing art.* Dallas, TX: Crescendo Publications.

Lessinger, L., & Salowe, A. (1997). *Game time: The educator's playbook for the new global economy.* Lancaster, PA: Technomic.

Levačić, R., & Glatter, R. (2001). Really good ideas? Developing evidence-informed policy and practice in educational leadership and management. *Educational Management and Administration, 29*(1), 5–25.

Levin, J. S. (2002). *Globalizing the community college.* New York: Palgrave.

Lindle, J., & Cibulka, J. (2006). Accountability. In F. English (Ed.), *Encyclopedia of educational leadership and administration* (pp. 2–12). Thousand Oaks, CA: Sage.

Lipman-Blumen, J. (2005). *The allure of toxic leaders.* New York: Oxford University Press.

Locker, J., & Cropley, M. (2004). Anxiety, depression and self-esteem in secondary school children: An investigation into the impact of Standard Assessment Tests (SATs) and other important school examinations. *School Psychology International, 25*(3), 333–345.

Lugg, C. (2000). *For God and country: Conservatism and American school policy.* New York: Peter Lang.

Lumby, J. (2006). Conceptualising diversity and leadership: Evidence from ten cases. *Educational Management and Administration, 34*(2), 151–165.

Lumby, J. (2007). Parent voice: Knowledge, values and viewpoint. *Improving Schools, 10*(3), 220–232.

Lumby, J., & Coleman, M. (2007). *Leadership and diversity: Challenging theory and practice in education.* Thousand Oaks, CA: Sage.

Lumby, J., & English, F. W. (2009). From simplicism to complexity in leadership identity and preparation: Exploring the lineage and dark secrets. *International Journal of Leadership in Education, 12*(2), 95–114.

Lumby, J., & Morrison, M. (2006). Partnership, conflict and gaming. *Journal of Education Policy, 21*(3), 323–341.

Lumby, J., & Morrison, M. (2009). Youth perspectives: Schooling, capabilities frameworks and human rights. *International Journal of Inclusive Education, 13*(6), 581–596.

MacIntyre, A. (1981). *After virtue* (3rd ed.). Notre Dame, IN: University of Notre Dame Press.

Manchester, W. (1978). *American Caesar: Douglas MacArthur 1880–1964.* Boston: Little, Brown.

Mangham, I. L. (1996). Some consequences of taking Gareth Morgan seriously. In D. Grant & C. Oswick (Eds.), *Metaphor and organizations* (pp. 21–36). London: Sage.

Marcellino, P. A. (2007). Reframing metaphors in business and education teams. *Journal of Education Administration, 45*(3), 289–314.

Markey, E. (2004). *The History of Theatre in Human Life.* Speech commemorating the fiftieth anniversary of Brown versus Board of Education. Retrieved March 31, 2010, from http://markey.house.gov/index.php?option=com_content&task=view&id=817&Itemid=141.

Marley, D., & Judd, J. (2009, September 11). Headteachers: Heads' £50,000 pay top-up. *The Times Educational Supplement.* Retrieved September 9, 2009, from http://www.tes.co.uk/Article.aspx?storycode=6022650.

McCreath, D., & Maclachlan, K. (1995). Realizing the virtual: New alliances in the market model education game. In A. Macbeth, D. McCreath, & J. Aitchison (Eds.), *Collaborate or compete? Educational partnerships in a market economy* (Ch. 6). London: Falmer.

Mead, G. H. (1934). *Mind, self and society: From the standpoint of a social behaviorist.* Chicago: University of Chicago Press.

Meckler, L. (2009, March 11). Obama seeks to expand merit pay for teachers. *The Wall Street Journal,* p. A6.

Micklethwait, J., & Wooldridge, A. (2009, April 7). God still isn't dead. *The Wall Street Journal,* p. A15.

Miller, B. (2004). The case against metaphor: An apologia. *Explorations in Nonfiction, 6*(2), 115–118. Retrieved April 5, 2010, from http://muse.jhu.edu/journals/fourth_genre_explorations_in_nonfiction/toc/fge6.2.html.

Milliken, J., & Colohan, G. (2004). Quality or control? Management in higher education. *Journal of Higher Education Policy and Management, 26*(3), 381–391.

Mintzberg, H. (1983). *Structure in fives: Designing effective organizations.* Englewood Cliffs, NJ: Prentice Hall.

Mintzberg, H. (2009, August 17). Executive briefing: What managers really do. *The Wall Street Journal,* p. R2.

Mongon, D., & Chapman, C. (2008). *Successful leadership for promoting the achievement of white working class pupils: A report prepared for the national union of teachers and national college for school leadership.* Nottingham: NCSL.

Morgan, G. (1986). *Images of organization.* Thousand Oaks, CA: Sage.

Moss, A. (1993). Commonplace-rhetoric and thought-patterns in early modern culture. In R. H. Roberts & J. M. Good (Eds.), *The recovery of rhetoric: Persuasive discourse and disciplinarity in the human sciences.* Charlottesville: University Press of Virginia.

Mulford, B., & Silins, H. (2003). Leadership for organisational learning and improved student outcomes—what do we know? *Cambridge Journal of Education, 33*(2), 175–195.

Munby, S. (2009). Steve Munby's speech to NCSL's Annual Leadership Conference. Nottingham, UK: NCSL. Retrieved April 5, 2010, from http://www.nationalcollege.org.uk/download?id=14986&filename=steve-munby-speech-conference-2009.pdf.

Murphy, J. (2002). Re-culturing the profession. In J. Murphy (Ed.), *The educational leadership challenge: Redefining leadership for the 21st century (National Society for the Study of Education Yearbooks, 101st, pt. 1).* Chicago: University of Chicago Press.

Nathan, J. (1999, October 7). Sony CEO's management style wasn't "made" in Japan. *The Wall Street Journal,* p. A30.

National Commission on Excellence in Education. (1983). *A nation at risk: The imperative for educational reform.* Washington, DC: US Department of Education.

National Union of Teachers. (2006). *National Union of Teachers survey: The roles and responsibilities of head teachers.* Retrieved January 19, 2009, from http://www.teachers.org.uk/resources/word/NUT-SURVEY-REP-ROLESRESPS-OF-HDTCHRS.doc.

Nestor-Baker, N., & Hoy, W. (2001). Tacit knowledge of school superintendents: Its nature, meaning, and content. *Educational Administration Quarterly, 37*(1), 86–129.

Ng, P. T. (2004). Students' perception of change in the Singapore education system. *Educational Research for Policy and Practice, 3,* 77–92.

Ng, P. T. (2007). Quality assurance in the Singapore education system in an era of diversity and innovation. *Educational Research for Policy and Practice, 6,* 235–247.

Nietzsche, F. (2008). *The complete works of Friedrich Nietzsche* (R. T. Gray, Trans.).Stanford, CA: Stanford University Press.

Nisbet, R. (1970). *History of the idea of progress.* New York: Basic Books.

Nussbaum, M. (1999). *Women and human development: The capabilities approach.* Cambridge, UK: Cambridge University Press.

O'Boyle, T. (1998). *At any cost: Jack Welch, General Electric, and the pursuit of profit.* New York: Vintage Books.

O'Connor, K. E. (2008). "You choose to care": Teachers, emotions and professional identity. *Teaching and Teacher Education, 24,* 117–126.

Obama, B. (2009). *Taking on education.* Retrieved October 19, 2009, from http://www.freireproject.org/blogs/obamas-education-speech-press-release.

Oberlechner, T., & Mayer-Schoenberger, V. (2002). *Through their own words: Towards new understanding of leadership through metaphors.* Retrieved March 29, 2010, from http://web.hks.harvard.edu/publications/workingpapers/citation.aspx?PubId=1133.

Odden, A., & Picus, L. (2004). *School finance: A policy perspective.* Boston: McGraw-Hill.

Office of the Press Secretary. (2004). President discusses education and changing job market, Central Dauphin High School, Harrisburg, Pennsylvania, February 12. Retrieved December 29, 2009, from http://www.whitehouse.gov/news/releases/2004/02/20040212–5.html.

Olssen, M., & Peters, M. (2005). Higher education and the knowledge economy: From the free market to knowledge capitalism. *Journal of Education Policy, 20*(3), 313–345.

Opfer, V. D. (2001). Charter schools and the panoptic effect of accountability. *Education and Urban Society, 33*(2), 201–215.

Ortega y Gasset, J. (1925). *The dehumanization of art and ideas about the novel.* Princeton, NJ: Princeton University Press.

Ortony, A. (1975). Why metaphors are necessary and not just nice. *Educational Theory, 25*(1), 45–53.

Orwell, G. (1945). *Animal farm.* New York: Harcourt Brace.

Orwell, G. (1950). *1984.* New York: Penguin.

Orwell, G. (1961). *George Orwell: Collected essays.* London: Secker & Warburg. (Original work published 1946)

Osler, A. (2004). Changing leadership and schools: Diversity, equality and citizenship. *Race Equality Teaching, 22*(3), 22–28.

Partnoy, F. (2003). *Infectious greed: How deceit and risk corrupted the financial markets.* New York: Henry Holt.

Pattison, S. (1997). *The faith of the managers: When management becomes religion.* London: Cassell.

Pattison, S. (2000). Recognizing leaders' hidden beliefs. In R. Banks & K. Powell (Eds.), *Faith in leadership* (pp. 169–184). San Francisco: Jossey-Bass.

Patton, G. S. (1975). *War as I knew it.* Boston: Houghton Mifflin.

Pereira, J. (2009, June 9). Steiff CEO is accused of rape. *The Wall Street Journal,* p. B5.

Perinbanayagam, R. S. (1985). *Signifying acts: Structure and meaning in everyday life.* Carbondale: Southern Illinois University Press.

Perrett, B. (1993). *Last stand! Famous battles against the odds.* London: Villars House.

Perryman, J. (2006). Panoptic performativity and school inspection regimes: Disciplinary mechanisms and life under special measures. *Journal of Education Policy, 21*(2), 147–161.

Phillips, A. (2005). Participation, inequality, self-interest. In G. Crozier & D. Reay (Eds.), *Activating participation: Parents and teachers working towards partnership* (Ch. 5). Stoke-on-Trent, UK: Trentham Books.

Pitino, R. (1997). *Success is a choice: Ten steps to overachieving in business and life.* New York: Broadway Books.

Plato (1973). *The phaedrus of Plato (Philosophy of Plato and Aristotle)* (W.H. Thompson, Ed.). New York: Arno Press.

Poletti, E. J. (2004). The gold in the heads of scientists: Metaphor and public sector reform. *Financial Accountability and Management, 20*(1), 19–38.

Pollitt, C. (1990). *Managerialism and the public services: The Anglo-American experience.* Oxford, UK: Blackwell.

Porter, G., & Kakabadse, N. K. (2006). HRM perspectives on addiction to technology and work. *Journal of Management Development, 25*(6), 535–560.

Powell, M. (2009, October 21). Thompson's role in schools post: A deft hand behind the scenes. *The New York Times,* pp. A1-A29.

Quantz, R. A., & Rogers, J. (1991). Rethinking transformative leadership: Toward democratic reform of schools [Electronic version]. *Journal of Education, 173*(3), 1–16.

Randle, K., & Brady, N. (1997). Further education and the new managerialism. *Journal of Further and Higher Education, 21*(2), 229–239.

Reay, D. (2001). Finding or losing yourself? Working class relationships to education. *Journal of Education Policy, 16*(4), 333–346.

Remove bad teachers, says adviser. (2007, November 10). *BBC News.* Retrieved March 29, 2010, from http://news.bbc.co.uk/2/hi/uk_news/education/7088383.stm.

Ready, set, go: Reviving America's schools. (2009, October 3). *The Economist, 393*(8651), 33–34.

The rich, the poor and the growing gap between them—Inequality in America. (2006, June 17). *The Economist, 379*(8482), pp. 28–30.

Riley, N. (2009, August 29). "We're in the venture philanthrophy business." The weekend interview with Eli Broad. *The Wall Street Journal,* p. A11.

Robinson, V. (2009, June 15). Warning on "sky-high" pay for Leeds headteachers. *Yorkshire Evening Post.* Retrieved September 9, 2009, from http://www.yorkshireeveningpost.co.uk/yourviews/Warning-on-39skyhigh39-pay-for.5365733.jp.

Robinson, V., & Timperley, H. (1996). Learning to be responsive: The impact of school choice and decentralization. *Educational Management and Administration, 24*(1), 65–78.

Rogers, J. (1985). *The dictionary of cliches.* New York: Wings Books.

Ross, T. (2009, June 23). £200,000 salary for headteachers who run merged school chains. *London Evening Standard.* Retrieved September 9, 2009, from http://www.thisislondon.co.uk/standard/article-23710849-200000-salary-for-headteachers-who-run-merged-school-chains.do.

Rusch, E. (2004). Gender and race in leadership preparation: A constrained discourse. *Educational Administration Quarterly, 40*(1), 16–48.

Russell, B. (1986). *Bertrand Russell on God and religion.* Amherst, NY: Prometheus Books.

Sallis, E. (1996). *Total quality management in education* (2nd ed.). London: Kogan Page.

Saltman, K. (2000). *Collateral damage: Corporatizing public schools—A threat to democracy.* Lanham, MD: Rowman & Littlefield.

Samier, E. (2005). Towards public administration as a humanities discipline: A humanistic manifesto. *Halduskultuur: Administrative Culture, 6,* 6–59.

Samier, E., & Lumby, J. (2010). Alienation, servility, and amorality: Relating Gogol's portrayal of bureaupathology to an accountability era. *Educational Management Administration & Leadership, 38,* 360–373.

Sammons, P., Hillman, J., & Mortimore, P. (1995). *Key characteristics of effective schools: A review of school effectiveness research.* London: Ofsted.

Sandars, N. K. (Trans.). (1960). *The epic of Gilgamesh.* London: Penguin.

Sawchuk, S. (2009, October 28). Duncan shares concerns over teacher prep. *Education Week,* 29(9), 1–12.

Schapper, A. (2009*). "Investing in a girl's education is like watering a neighbor's tree": A case study on promoting the rights of the girl child at the local level in Bangladesh.* Paper presented at the annual meeting of the ISA's annual convention, New York. Retrieved November 4, 2009, from www.allacademic.com/meta/p312297_index.html.

Schumpeter, J. (1950). *Capitalism, socialism and democracy* (as cited in Chernow). New York: Harper Torchbooks. (Original work published 1942)

Schweitzer, A. (1965). *The teaching of reverence for life.* New York: Holt, Rinehart & Winston.

Selwyn, N. (2000). The National Grid for Learning: Panacea or panopticon? *British Journal of Sociology of Education, 21*(2), 243–255.

Sen, A. (1984). *Resources, values and development.* Cambridge, MA: Harvard University Press.

Shain, F., & Gleeson, D. (1999). Under new management: Changing conceptions of teacher professionalism and policy in the further education sector. *Journal of Education Policy, 14*(4), 445–462.

Shakespeare, W. (1964). A midsummer night's dream. In P. Alexander (Ed.), *The complete works of Shakespeare* (pp. 198–222). London: Collins.

Shakespeare, W. (1964). Hamlet. In P. Alexander (Ed.), *The complete works of Shakespeare* (pp. 1028–1072). London: Collins.

Shipman, N., Queen, J., & Peel, H. (2007). *Transforming school leadership with ISLLC and ELCC.* Larchmont, NY: Eye on Education.

Simkins, T. (2000). Education reform and managerialism: Comparing the experience of schools and colleges. *Journal of Education Policy, 15*(3), 317–332.

Simon, H. (1945). *Administrative theory.* New York: Macmillan.

Simon, S. (2009a, April 13). Education board in Texas faces curbs. *The Wall Street Journal,* p. A6.

Simon, S. (2009b, August 17). Hard-hit schools try public-relations push. *The Wall Street Journal,* p. A3.

Sims, A. (2003). *Symptoms in the mind: An introduction to descriptive psychopathology* (3rd ed.). London: Saunders.

Skinner, B. F. (1958). Teaching machines. *Science, 128*(3330), 969–977.

Skinner, Q. (1991). Introduction: The return of grand theory. In Q. Skinner (Ed.), *The return of grand theory in the human sciences* (pp. 1–20). Cambridge, UK: Cambridge University Press.

Slater, J. (2003, June 27). Specialists scoop £4m software deal. *The Times Educational Supplement.* Retrieved January 17, 2009, from http://www.tes.co.uk/article.aspx?storycode=381415.

Slee, R. (1994). Finding a student voice in school reform: Student disaffection, pathologies of disruption and educational reform. *International Studies in the Sociology of Education, 4*(2), 147–172.

Smith, M. L., Miller-Kahn, L., Heinecke, W., & Jarvis, P. F. (2004). *Political spectacle and the fate of American schools.* New York: RoutledgeFalmer.

Smyth, J. (1989). Supervision-as-school reform: A critical perspective. *Journal of Education Policy*, 4(4), 343–361.

Sparkes, R. A. (1999, September–October). *Lies, damned lies and school performance indicators.* Paper presented at the Scottish Educational Research Association Annual Conference, University of Dundee, UK.

Spears, R. (1997). *Hip hot: A dictionary of 10,000 American slang expressions.* New York: Gramercy Books.

Spillane, J. P., Halverson, R., & Diamond, J. B. (2004). Towards a theory of leadership practice: A distributed perspective. *Journal of Curriculum Studies, 36*(1), 3–34.

Stanislavski, C., & Reynolds Hapgood, E. (Trans.). (1989). *An actor prepares.* New York: Routledge. (Original work published 1936)

Starratt, R. J. (1993). *The drama of leadership.* London: The Falmer Press.

Steer, R., Spours, K., Hodgson, A., Finlay, I., Coffield, F., Edward, S., et al. (2007). "Modernisation" and the role of policy levers in the learning and skills sector. *Journal of Vocational Education and Training, 59*(2), 175–192.

Stewart, J. (1996). *Local government today.* London: Local Government Management Board.

Strobridge, T. (1986). White Rose of the skies. *Military History, 3*(3), 14–17, 61.

Sturdy, A., Brocklehurst, M., Winstanley, D., & Littlejohns, M. (2006). Management as a (self) confidence trick: Management ideas, education and identity work. *Organization, 13*(6), 841–860.

Summers, H. G. (1982). *On strategy: A critical analysis of the Vietnam War.* Navato, CA: Presidio Press.

Sun Tzu. (1988). *The art of war* (T. Cleary, Trans.). London: Shambala.

Swanson, D. R. (1979). Towards a psychology of metaphor. In S. Sacks (Ed.), *On metaphor* (pp. 161-164). Chicago: University of Chicago Press.

Taylor, F. (1911). *The principles of scientific management.* New York: Harper & Brothers.

Taylor Fitz-Gibbon, C. (1996). *Monitoring education: Indicators, quality and effectiveness.* London: Cassell.

Obama's Education Opening (2009, March 14). *The Wall Street Journal*, p. A8.

THES Jobs. (2009, October). *Times Higher Education.* Retrieved October 22, 2009, from http://www.timeshighereducation.co.uk/jobs_jobdetails.asp?ac=72091.

Thompson, V. (n.d.). *The impact of home access to learning technologies.* Leatherhead, UK: e-Learning Foundation. Retrieved March 29, 2010, from http://74.125.113.132/search?q=cache:n7Sss0sK0bwJ:www.teachernet.gov.uk/_doc/10407/Event%2520Presentation%2520eLearning%2520Foundation%2520impact%2520of%2520Home%2520Access%2520to%2520Learning%2520Technologies.ppt+The+impact+of+home+access+to+learning+technologies.+Leatherhead:+E+Learning+Foundation.&cd=3&hl=en&ct=clnk&gl=us&client=safari.

Thrupp, P. M. (1999). *Schools making a difference: Let's be realistic!* Buckingham: Open University Press.

Tod, C. (1974). Administrative diseases: Some types of dysfunctionality in administration. *Public Administration, 52*(Autumn), 439–454.

Toffler, B. (2003). *Final accounting: Ambition, greed, and the fall of Arthur Andersen.* New York: Broadway Books.

Torres, K. (2009, September 10). Panel: Suspend school officials. *The Atlanta Constitution,* pp. A1, A7.

Trnavčevič, A., & Vaupot, S. R. (2009). Exploring aspiring principals' perceptions of principalship: A Slovenian case study. *Educational Management Administration Leadership, 37*(1), 85–105.

Tsoukas, H. (1991). The missing link: A transformational view of metaphors in organisational science. *The Academy of Management Review, 16*(3), 566–585.

Turbayne, C. M. (1962). *The myth of metaphor.* New Haven, CT: Yale University Press.

Turchiano, J. (2004). William J. Bennett. In J. Newfield, & M. Jacobson (Eds.), *American monsters: 44 rats, black hats, and plutocrats* (pp. 23–32). New York: Thunder's Mouth Press.

Tyack, D. (2007). *Seeking common ground: Public schools in a diverse society.* Cambridge, MA: Harvard University Press.

Usher, R., & Edwards, R. (1994). *Postmodernism and education.* London: Routledge.

Van den Bulte, C. (1994). Metaphor at work. In G. Laurent, G. L. Lillien, & B. Pras (Eds.), *Research traditions in marketing* (pp. 405–425). Boston: Kluwer.

Vranica, S., & Futterman, M. (2009, August 5). NFL teams with Procter & Gamble in a play for new kinds of sponsors. *The Wall Street Journal,* p. B5.

Walker, B. G. (1983). *The woman's encyclopedia of myths and secrets.* San Francisco: Harper Collins.

Watson, C. (1981). *Results-oriented managing: The key to effective performance.* Reading, MA: Addison-Wesley.

Weber, M. (1970). The Protestant Sects and the Spirit of Capitalism. In H. Gerth, & C. Mills (Eds.), *From Max Weber: Essays in sociology.* New York: Oxford University Press. (Original work published 1946)

Weber, M. (1991). *The sociology of religion.* Boston: Beacon Press. (Original work published 1922)

Weber, M. (1992). *The sociology of religion.* Boston: Beacon Press. (Original work published 1922)

Weber, M. (2003). *The Protestant ethic and the spirit of capitalism.* Mineola, NY: Dover Publications. (Original work published 1958)

Webster's seventh new collegiate dictionary (1971). Springfield, MA: G. & C. Merriam.

Weinberg, N. (2003, October 6). Educating Eli. *Forbes,* pp. 106–110.

Wells, A. S. (2009, March 2). From Obama's Generation: The audacious hope of more racially diverse public schools. *Education Week.* Retrieved December 30, 2009, from http://www.edweek.org/login.html?source= http://www.edweek.org/ew/articles/2009/03/04/23wells_ep.h28.html&destination= http://www.edweek.org/ew/articles/2009/03/04/23wells_ep.h28.html&levelId=2100.

West, A., & Pennell, H. (2007). How new is New Labour? The quasimarket and English schools, 1997 to 2001. *British Journal of Educational Studies, 50*(2), 206–224.

Whitehouse, M. (2009, November 3). Crisis compels economists to reach for new paradigm. *The Wall Street Journal,* pp. A1, A18.

Whitty, G. (1994). *Deprofessionalising teaching? Recent developments in teacher education in England.* Deakin: Australian College of Education.

Wilkinson, G. (2005). Workforce remodeling and formal knowledge: The erosion of teachers' professional jurisdiction in English schools. *School Leadership and Management, 25*(5), 421–439.

Wilson, V., & Hall, J. (2002). Running twice as fast? A review of the research literature on teachers' stress. *Scottish Educational Review, 34*(2), 175–187

Wise, A. (1979). *Legislated learning: The bureaucratization of the American classroom.* Berkeley: University of California Press.

Womack, J. P., Jones, D. T., & Roos, D. (1990). *The machine that changed the world: The story of lean production.* New York: Rawson & Associates.

Woolgar, S. (2000). Virtual society? Beyond the hype. *The Source.* Retrieved March 31, 2010, from http://www.thesourcepublishing.co.uk/thesourcepublishing.html.

World Health Organization (1946). Constitution of the World Health Organization. *Official Record of the World Health Questionnaire, 2,* 100.

Wrigley, T. (2004). 'School effectiveness': The problem of reductionism. *British Educational Research Journal, 30*(2), 227–244.

Yarker, P. (2005). On not being a teacher: The professional and personal costs of workforce remodeling. *Forum (for Promoting 3–19 Comprehensive Education), 47*(2–3), 169–174.

Youell, B. (2005). Assessment, evaluation and inspection in schools: A psychodynamic perspective. *Infant Observation, 8*(1), 59–68.

Zaslow, J. (2004, September 20). Win! Win! Kill! Kill! What works in the locker room may work in the corporate conference room. Or maybe not. *The Wall Street Journal,* p. R7.

Index

CORWIN

A SAGE Company

The Corwin logo—a raven striding across an open book—represents the union of courage and learning. Corwin is committed to improving education for all learners by publishing books and other professional development resources for those serving the field of PreK–12 education. By providing practical, hands-on materials, Corwin continues to carry out the promise of its motto: **"Helping Educators Do Their Work Better."**